Emanuela Prinzivalli
The Gospel and the Church

Hans-Lietzmann-Vorlesungen

Edited on behalf of the Berlin-
Brandenburg Academy of Sciences and Humanities
by Katharina Bracht and Christoph Markschies

Volume 23

Emanuela Prinzivalli

The Gospel and the Church

—

The Words of Jesus in the Process of Ecclesiastical Institutionalization in Rome (First to Fifth Centuries)

DE GRUYTER

ISBN 978-3-11-157397-7
e-ISBN (PDF) 978-3-11-157415-8
e-ISBN (EPUB) 978-3-11-157500-1
ISSN 1861-6011

Library of Congress Control Number: 2025930977

Bibliographic information published by the Deutsche Nationalbibliothek
The Deutsche Nationalbibliothek lists this publication in the Deutsche Nationalbibliografie;
detailed bibliographic data are available on the Internet at http://dnb.dnb.de.

© 2025 Walter de Gruyter GmbH, Berlin/Boston, Genthiner Straße 13, 10785 Berlin
Typesetting: Integra Software Services Pvt. Ltd.

www.degruyter.com
Questions about General Product Safety Regulation:
productsafety@degruyterbrill.com

Foreword

Advent in the 2020s – reminiscent expectation of the birth of Christ and hopeful expectation of the second coming of Christ. The Advent season, during which the Hans Lietzmann Lectures traditionally take place, provides an opportunity to take a look at the time of the Church, which lies between the birth and the second coming of Christ and now spans almost 2000 years.

Emanuela Prinzivalli addressed this topic in the twenty-eighth Hans Lietzmann Lecture in 2022. She focuses on a particularly crucial point: On the transition from Jesus of Nazareth to the Church, i.e. the transition from the itinerant Jewish teacher with his potentially subversive message of the dawning kingdom of God to the ecclesiastical institution, which, like all institutions, has an essential interest in stability and self-assertion. Seen in this light, the starting point and the (provisional) end of the process of the institutionalization of Christianity stand in a fundamental contradiction to one another, and yet they are closely linked in terms of content. In her study, Emanuela Prinzivalli brings both aspects together by asking which words of Jesus were used by representatives of the ancient church, in what context, in what way and with what aim. She asks which strategies were used to adapt the message of Jesus to the needs of the Church as an institution. In doing so, she focuses on the Church of Rome in (Late) Antiquity as an example, beginning with *First Letter of Clement* until Boniface the First and Leo the Great.

With this question, which combines New Testament studies and ancient church history, Emanuela Prinzivalli ties in with the research of the church historian Hans Lietzmann (1875–1942), after whom the lecture series is named. He held the Jena Chair of Church History from 1905 to 1923 before succeeding Adolf von Harnack in Berlin. Hans Lietzmann combined the history of ancient Christianity in an outstanding way not only with classical philology and archaeology, but also with New Testament scholarship.

Emanuela Prinzivalli has been Professor of Christianity and Church History at the Sapienza University in Rome since 2000. Her research focuses on ancient church history, ancient Christian literary history, the exegesis of the Church Fathers, and a gender perspective on these "classical" topics. Four authors, among others, are at the center of her interest: Hippolytus of Rome (beginning of third century), Origen (d. 254 CE), Origen's first critic Methodius of Olympus (d. 311 CE), who lived in the period of the forty-year great peace before the last great persecution of Christians by Diocletian, but also Origen's faithful follower Didymus the Blind (d. 398 CE), who was born around the year when Methodius died.

Emanuela Prinzivalli is particularly concerned with the biblical reception of these authors. Here again, a particular focus is on the exegesis of the Psalms. In the 1990s, she critically edited Origen's homilies on the 36th, 37th and 38th Psalms for the renowned series *Biblioteca Patristica* (vol. 18, 1991) and *Sources Chrétiennes* (vol. 411, 1995). This work was crowned when she was involved in the critical edition of a sensational manuscript find in the Bavarian State Library: When twelve years ago the original Greek text of twenty-nine homilies on the Psalms by Origen was discovered in the twelfth century Codex Monacensis Graecus 314, Emanuela Prinzivalli edited the homilies on Psalm 36, which until then were known only in Rufinus' Latin translation, for the *editio princeps* in the series *Die Griechischen Christlichen Schriftsteller der ersten Jahrhunderte* (N.F. 19, 2015, 113–172). This discovery also is of special interest because it made it possible to take "a fresh look at Rufinus as translator", to quote one of the titles of her numerous essays (*Origeniana Undecima*, ed. A.-Chr. Jacobsen, *Bibliotheca ephemeridum theologicarum Lovaniensium* 279, 2016, 247–276).

Personally, I met Emanuela Prinzivalli for the first time almost twenty years ago in Rome. I sought contact with her because I had written my dissertation on the same Methodius of Olympus who is a focus of her research. The aim of my trip to Rome was also to meet two scholars from her circle of students who were working on Methodius as well: Miroslaw Mejzner, SAC, and M. Benedetta Selene Zorzi, OSB, who at that stage were cooperating in translating Methodius' writing *De resurrectione* into Italian (published as Metodio di Olimpo: La risurrezione, *Collana di testi patristici* 216, 2010).

We met for a research discussion on Methodius and other patristic topics. When Emanuela Prinzivalli noticed that a rather diverse group was sitting in her office – Miroslaw Mejzner a Roman Catholic priest from Poland, Benedetta Selene Zorzi an Italian Benedictine nun and myself a Protestant ordained minister from Germany – she spontaneously invited us into her lecture room for a panel discussion with the students on the church's understanding of ministry. For me, this was a key experience of how the study of patristics, the return to the common roots of Christianity, can prepare the ground for ecumenical dialog and experiences in our present day.

The Hans Lietzmann Lecture presented here to the interested public is also about the common roots of Christianity: about the words of Jesus which played a special role during the institutionalization of the church in the first five centuries.

This foreword ends with thanks. I would like to thank cordially Dr. Albrecht Döhnert and the publishing house De Gruyter Brill which sponsors the Hans Lietzmann Lectures and publishes them in this small but excellent series, as well as my research assistant Maja Menzel, who prepared the manuscript for printing. I would also like to express my sincere thanks to my Berlin colleague and co-editor Christoph Markschies for the always excellent cooperation.

Jena, December 2024   Katharina Bracht

Contents

Foreword — V

Introduction — 1

1 What words of Jesus? — 3

2 The first three centuries — 6
    2.1   The so-called *First Letter of Clement to the Corinthians*: many words of Jesus — **6**
    2.2   Callixtus and the weeds — **8**
    2.3   Stephen and the strange interpretation of Mt 16:18–19 — **10**

3 After Constantine: a summary table — 13

4 The silence of Anastasius and Liberius — 15

5 Julius the First and the Roman *agape* — 16

6 The typologies of the *logia* of Jesus quoted by the bishops — 18

7 From Damasus to Siricius: the perfecting of the decretal letters — 20
    7.1   Damasus and the *Ad Gallos* — **20**
    7.2   Siricius and the decretal to Himerius — **21**

8 The paradoxes of Innocent and Zosimus — 24

9 The homilies of Leo the Great — 29

Conclusion — 35

Bibliography — 37

Introduction

I reflected a great deal about the topic I wished to propose for this lecture,[1] having the desire to best honor the memory of Hans Lietzmann. I asked myself whether I should not speak on a question that is very much alive now: the methodology of historical research in the field of Christianity.[2] But I think that every new perspective which integrates the necessary philological and historical perspectives in the analysis of texts remains somewhat abstract if it does not take on a concrete form through a focus on a particular object. Furthermore, I considered the fact that Lietzmann was also a great New Testament scholar. So, I decided to present an initial search which starts from the following question, formulated in the most general possible way: to what extent were the words of Jesus of Nazareth remembered by the ancient Church as a public institution? What phrases among those words of Jesus that have come down to us are the most mentioned and made use of? And in what contexts and for what purpose are they spoken again by the Church?

---

[1] I thank professors Katharina Bracht and Christoph Markschies, two colleagues dear to me: we have a long-standing friendship and common research interests.
[2] If I had decided to develop a discussion on the current state of history of early Christianity, I would have chosen, among many others, two main methodological trajectories. First trajectory: the multiple opportunities given by the integration of the historical perspective with that of the human sciences. I offer just a few examples of the gain that comes from valorising such an integration: *a)* the critical rethinking of the category of space. See, for example, E. Smith, *Foucault's Heterotopia in Christian Catacombs*; E.R. Urciuoli, *La religione urbana*; *b)* the impact of the so-called "Iconic/Pictorial Turn," which aims to integrate image and word, on which, regarding the history of Christianity, see A. Monaci and A. Nicolotti (eds.), "Vedere e guardare attraverso le parole"; T. Canella (ed.), "La Memoria e l'Immagine." Also the important volume of Ch. Markschies, *Gottes Körper*, 41–56; 113–143; 353–372, contains useful insights in this sense; *c)* the application of the category of gender in historical investigation: J.W. Scott, "Gender. A Useful Category of Historical Analysis"; Ead., "Unanswered Questions." I will give just one example for studies on ancient Christianity: M.Y. MacDonald and C. Osiek, *A Woman's Place. House Churches in Earliest Christianity*; *d)* the relationship with Network science: I. Czachesz (ed.), "Network Science in Biblical Studies." However, we must not forget the problem, traditional in studies, of the relationship between theology and the history of the Church: see now C. Kampmann et al. (eds.), *Kirchengeschichte. Historisches Spezialgebiet und/ oder Theologische Disziplin.*

Second Trajectory: the meaning of the study of Christianity in the era of globalization. Ph. Jenkins is a pioneer of this perspective of studies: Ph. Jenkins, *The Next Christendom*; Id., *The New Faces of Christianity*; for a historiographical balance sheet: J. Bruner, *How to Study Global Christianity*; M. Pesce's thoughts on the matter are radical but interesting: M. Pesce, "Alla ricerca di un nuovo schema mentale." I hope to be able to show the fruitfulness of these two trajectories in the drafting of a forthcoming, synthetic history of ancient Christianity.

I hope that these questions do not sound too naïve:³ I do think that asking them is useful since they touch on a problem central to many contemporary studies, namely, the process of selection and construction of memory.⁴

In this particular case, I want to see how and why an institution such as the Church and its tradition utilizes the memory of Jesus, who is the very cause of its existence. In this sense, it is particularly interesting to look at the Church of the first centuries in order to verify the impact of institutionalization on the reception of the Gospel message.

For a first survey, I will concentrate on the Church in Rome, most of all because of the important role that Rome played even from the first century among various groups of Christians and, whether for good or ill, that it continued to play for all of Western Christianity.⁵ I will deal with the topic up to the time of Boniface the First (418–422), as this will allow me to give a sort of provisional completeness to my lecture. I will, however, make a chronological and literary incursion outside of these parameters in taking up the first homiletic *corpus* preserved in the Roman Church, that of Pope Leo the Great (440–461). This will enable a comparison with previous sources and illustrate any differences between the homiletic mode of expression with reference to the memory of Jesus and what is said and done in official letters.

---

3 I rather hope (maybe in a utopian way) that, if these pages of mine turn out to be useful and interesting to readers, we can start a diachronic research (which obviously requires the contribution of many scholars) on the relationship between the words of Jesus and the various ecclesiastical institutions. I formulated a first proposal, in this sense, during my public lecture at Sapienza, organized by my colleague Tessa Canella, on September 28, 2021.

4 Current studies on memory, which is a creative and selective process, start from M. Halbwachs, *Les cadres sociaux de la mémoire*. Understanding the functioning of collective memory is fundamental for the reconstruction of traditions on Jesus and early Christianity. See, for example, S. Butticaz and E. Norelli (eds.), *Memory and Memories in Early Christianity*; R. Aguirre, "La segunda generación y la conservación de la memoria de Jesús." For the following period: Id., *La memoria. Forme e finalità del ricordare nel cristianesimo antico*. The first step for the preservation of memory was the use of eyewitnesses: S. Byrskog, *Story as History—History as Story*. J. Assmann's *Das kulturelle Gedächtnis* is a classic for the study of cultural perpetuation, that is, the establishment of tradition. For the reconstruction of the scientific discourse on memory starting from the end of the nineteenth century see C. Di Pasquale, *Antropologia della memoria*.

5 For the first three centuries of Christianity in Rome see: P. Lampe, *From Paul to Valentinus*. See also: E. Prinzivalli, *Il cristianesimo antico fra tradizioni e traduzioni* (Prima parte: *Intorno alla Chiesa di Roma*). For an updated synthesis of the various competing factions in Rome in the second century see F. Berno, *L'Atto di Pietro e le origini della comunità cristiana di Roma*, 85–101. On the ideological construction of presbyters as an ideal category for the transmission of the right faith, in Rome and elsewhere see: E. Norelli, "Dai presbiteri d'Asia agli episcopi di Roma." C. Pietri's volume *Roma christiana* is of centrale importance for the study of Christian Rome in late antiquity.

1 What words of Jesus?

I need now to clarify what I mean by "the words of Jesus." I will take up only the words of Jesus contained in the canonical Gospels[6] (or in traditions also present in these gospels) since they have a normative value and, therefore, starting roughly from the second half of the second century, have the highest level of authority. But this is not all: in order to limit even further which words of Jesus I intend to refer to, I need to recognize two other considerations that I will trace out quickly here.

First consideration: Jesus of Nazareth was a Jewish, itinerant preacher.[7] At the center of his message is the announcement of the Kingdom of God. His authority is of a charismatic character, that is, it is founded on his direct legitimization by God and not from his belonging to the class of the religious authority recognized by the society and institutions of the Judaism of his time. Now, looking at the modality by which Jesus spoke of the Kingdom of God and its coming, we see that he reformulates the foundation of human interaction. Namely, in the emphasis on mutual forgiveness and even love of one's enemies, there is a very strong ethical element which he presents as in continuity with or, even more, accentuating the Hebrew vision of God as the agent of a system of values (think particularly of the vision of God in Deuteronomy).[8]

This ethical refoundation of human interaction is not, however, an end in itself, but rather is ultimately directed towards an eschatological/apocalyptic end.[9] That is, it is directed towards an imminent change which God will bring about within humanity. Therefore, *metanoia* is required as a response to the gift of the imminent Kingdom of God, for the sake of receiving the reality of God, who will overturn any earthly power of oppression. Think of the first words spoken by

---

[6] For the English translation I will use the *New Revised Standard Version Updated Edition* (NRSVue). In a few cases, I will translate directy the biblical quotes from the different authors, reporting also their original texts.
[7] Jesus' itinerant manner continued to be important to an early generation of followers: G. Theissen, *Die Jesusbewegung*, passim; see also A. Destro and M. Pesce, *Encounters with Jesus*, passim.
[8] P. Sacchi, *Storia del Secondo Tempio*, offers an excellent overview on this matter; see also D. G. Firth and P.S. Johnston (eds.), *Interpreting Deuteronomy*.
[9] It appears to me that there is a majority consensus on this point among scholars of various confessions. I mention two as examples: D.C. Allison jr., *Constructing Jesus*, 156–164: the Presbyterian Allison, despite a methodological approach that challenges the criteria of authenticity, confirms the conviction of his previous volume *Jesus of Nazareth. Millenarian Prophet*. The Catholic priest Meier, who instead is based on the criteria of authenticity, has the same conviction: J.P. Meier, *A Marginal Jew*, 289–397.

Jesus in the Gospel of Mark (1:15): "The time is fulfilled, and the kingdom of God has come near; repent, and believe in the good news".[10] Remember also the Beatitudes in their Lucan formulation—"Blessed are you who are hungry now, for you will be filled. Blessed are you who weep now, for you will laugh" (Lk 6:21)—which in Luke's version always correspond to the so-called "woes": "But woe to you who are rich, for you have received your consolation. Woe to you who are full now, for you will be hungry. Woe to you who are laughing now, for you will mourn and weep" (Lk 6:24–25).[11]

As is evident from these verses, the message of the Gospel has an inextricable element of protest against the lived reality of its time and stands in contrast to any contemporary oppressive power. These are the words (the preaching of the Kingdom of God, the consequent *metanoia* required of human beings on the order of love and mutual forgiveness which in the end produces a new modality for human interaction) which historians consider the most likely to date back to the authentic preaching of Jesus. I will concentrate, then, on the words from the Gospels that come together in the Synoptic tradition and speak of the Kingdom of God, of the interaction of God with humanity, the parables that illustrate the Kingdom of God: that is, those which in some traditions were considered to have in and of themselves salvific value (see the *Gospel of Thomas*).

Second consideration: After the death of Jesus, the person of Jesus Christ becomes central to the message of evangelization—at least for the most common model of evangelization—and therefore also to the act of conversion. From this trajectory, which we could call largely Pauline-Johannine, there developed the conviction that the Jewish man Jesus was also God. Following from this came the problem that such a conviction conflicts with the proclamation of the one God in Judaism of the time (which we call today "Monotheism"). Among many of the first followers, then, evangelization focused on the person of Jesus himself as a saving reality. That is, Jesus as one not merely sent by God, but who is himself God.

Consequently, I will not speak of those words of Jesus which serve to substantiate or justify faith in Jesus Christ as God and which enter into the controversies that had already begun in the second century.[12] To take an example from the Roman sources: one of the few literary remains that come down to us from the

---

[10] Cf. R. Aguirre, "Jesús y el tiempo," 93–112.
[11] The "woes" have a secondary character: they can come either from tradition or from Luke. According to Bovon, there are more convicing arguments supporting that they are Luke's work: F. Bovon, *Das Evangelium nach Lukas*, 300.
[12] The issue of the role that considering Jesus as a God has had in the separation between Christians and Jews and in the creation of two different religious systems is debated. For the role of the fourth century Trinitarian controversies in this regard see E. Fiano, *Three Powers in Heaven*.

bishops of Rome from before the time of Nicaea is a long fragment of a letter by Dionysius of Rome (259–267) to Dionysius of Alexandria. The latter was accused by some of the faithful of his church of not considering the Son to be *homoousios* with the Father.[13] Dionysius of Rome cites the words of Jesus explicitly only two times—both times from the Gospel of John, which, as we know, is the more theological of the Gospels—in order to prove that the Son is not separate from the Father (as Dionysius of Alexandria was accused of holding) and that there is no need to divide the "wonderful and divine monad" into three separate gods since Jesus says: "The Father and I are one." (Jn 10:30), and "Believe me that I am in the Father and the Father is in me" (Jn 14:11). It is this type of quotation which was used in theological controversy which I have excluded from my lecture. In the Synoptic Gospels this sort of statement is, in fact, rare, while the Gospel of John is full of them.

---

[13] L. Abramowski, "Dionys von Rom [†268] und Dionys von Alexandrien (†264/5) in den arianischen Streitigkeiten des 4. Jahrhunderts," 240–272 believes that the few remaining fragments of Dionysius and the letter of Dionysius of Rome are a falsification carried out shortly before the Council of Serdica (343), in view of a possible compromise between Nicenes and anti-Nicenes. On the contrary, Simonetti expresses himself in favor of authenticity, through a precise refutation of Abramowski's arguments: M. Simonetti, "Aspetti della cristologia del III secolo. Dionigi di Alessandria," 37–65.

2 The first three centuries

2.1 The so-called *First Letter of Clement to the Corinthians*: many words of Jesus

Now, we can finally come to the argument at hand. For the period before Nicaea, the "official" sources (taking into account the approximation that such a term should have, especially with reference to the first two centuries) can be counted on one hand, while the amount after Nicaea is abundant. Of what sources are we speaking? Letters, with only one exception. The letters sent from the Church of Rome—from its bishop to various conciliar assemblies, or to other bishops and clerics, or to the emperor—all have (with some exceptions) a more or less higher level of officiality. From a certain point in history, far after the Constantinian age, the so-called "decretal" letters will acquire an even normative value.

The first text to examine is the so-called *First Letter of Clement to the Corinthians* from the end of the first century. The letter was in fact written by "the church of God that lives as a foreigner in Rome," and is attributed by tradition to a Clement (a rather common name), in response to the church of Corinth, particularly to those faithful who had requested assistance from Rome after the deposition of some of their presbyters for reasons that are unknown. In any event, the letter from Rome considers the depositions as the result of the vanity and divisions within the church and a tragic *stasis* ("rebellion"). We are, of course, in a period before the formation of the New Testament canon, before the wide diffusion of the Gospels and maybe even before the creation of some of them. In this letter, which presents a Christology that stands between the low and high, the words of Jesus are amply recorded: the letter presents a collection of *logia* of Jesus that are found in a similar or nearly identical form in the Synoptic Gospels but were likely transmitted to the author of the letter through an independent tradition, in a form that facilitated memorization. The setting of the letter takes up the deliberative rhetorical style (or συμβουλευτικόν), which intends to move the hearer to make a more advantageous decision. In this case, it is to reinstate the deposed presbyters, and the words of Jesus which are cited have that outcome as their purpose. The language of conversion is constantly present in the letter, adapted to a very specific situation: the conversion of the Corinthians consists in letting go of their fights and disagreements so as to follow the will of God and not their own. In this, they must follow the example of Jesus, the model of humility, meekness, and kindness.

There is little material in the letter by which to examine the merits of the historical situation itself, and so we will not deal with that here.[14] I will only say that regardless of how one considers the use which the author makes of the words of Jesus, the letter contains an anthology of the sayings of Jesus of such quality and quantity that we will not find in any of the texts that follow. We are also far from any presumption on the part of the Church of Rome to impose a solution: the writer relies rather on persuasive rhetoric and it is with this lens that the citations of the words of Jesus are explained. See Table 1.

Table 1: Comparison of the *First Letter of Clement of Rome to the Corinthians* and the sayings in the Gospels of Matthew and Luke.

First Letter of Clement 13	*The Tradition of Matthew and Luke*
[. . .] Especially should we remember the words which the Lord spoke, when He taught clemency and longsuffering:	
For He spoke thus: Be merciful, that you may receive mercy (Ἐλεᾶτε, ἵνα ἐλεηθῆτε).	Mt 5:7: Blessed are the merciful, for they will receive mercy (μακάριοι οἱ ἐλεήμονες, ὅτι αὐτοὶ ἐλεηθήσονται).
Forgive, that you may be forgiven (ἀφίετε, ἵνα ἀφεθῇ ὑμῖν);	Mt 6:14-15: For if you forgive others their trespasses, your heavenly Father will also forgive you, but if you do not forgive others, neither will your Father forgive your trespasses (Ἐὰν γὰρ ἀφῆτε τοῖς ἀνθρώποις τὰ παραπτώματα αὐτῶν, ἀφήσει καὶ ὑμῖν ὁ πατὴρ ὑμῶν ὁ οὐράνιος· ἐὰν δὲ μὴ ἀφῆτε τοῖς ἀνθρώποις, οὐδὲ ὁ πατὴρ ὑμῶν ἀφήσει τὰ παραπτώματα ὑμῶν).
As you do, so shall it be done to you (ὡς ποιεῖτε, οὕτω ποιηθήσεται ὑμῖν·);	Lk 6:31: Do to others as you would have them do to you (καὶ καθὼς θέλετε ἵνα ποιῶσιν ὑμῖν οἱ ἄνθρωποι, ποιεῖτε αὐτοῖς ὁμοίως). Cf. Mt 7:12: In everything do to others as you would have them do to you, for this is the Law and the Prophets (Πάντα οὖν ὅσα ἐὰν θέλητε ἵνα ποιῶσιν ὑμῖν οἱ ἄνθρωποι, οὕτως καὶ ὑμεῖς ποιεῖτε αὐτοῖς· οὗτος γάρ ἐστιν ὁ νόμος καὶ οἱ προφῆται).

---

14 Cf. E. Prinzivalli, "La prima lettera di Clemente ai Corinzi," 89–117.

Table 1 (continued)

As you give, so shall it be given to you (ὡς δίδοτε, οὕτως δοθήσεται ὑμῖν·);	Lk 6:38a: give, and it will be given to you (δίδοτε, καὶ δοθήσεται ὑμῖν).
	Lk 6:38b: A good measure, pressed down, shaken together, running over, will be put into your lap (καλὸν πεπιεσμένον σεσαλευμένον ὑπερεκχυννόμενον δώσουσιν εἰς τὸν κόλπον ὑμῶν).
As you judge, so shall you be judged (ὡς κρίνετε, οὕτως κριθήσεσθε);	Lk 6:37a: Do not judge, and you will not be judged (Καὶ μὴ κρίνετε, καὶ οὐ μὴ κριθῆτε·); do not condemn, and you will not be condemned. Forgive, and you will be forgiven (καὶ μὴ καταδικάζετε, καὶ οὐ μὴ καταδικασθῆτε).
As you are kind, so shall you be treated kindly (ὡς χρηστεύεσθε, οὕτως χρηστευθήσεται ὑμῖν·); for the measure you give so will be the measure you get (ᾧ μέτρῳ μετρεῖτε, ἐν αὐτῷ μετρηθήσεται ὑμῖν).	Mt 7:1-2: Do not judge, so that you may not be judged. For the judgment you give will be the judgment you get and the measure you give will be the measure you get (Μὴ κρίνετε, ἵνα μὴ κριθῆτε· ἐν ᾧ γὰρ κρίματι κρίνετε κριθήσεσθε, καὶ ἐν ᾧ μέτρῳ μετρεῖτε μετρηθήσεται ὑμῖν).
	Lk 6:38c: for the measure you give will be the measure you get back (ᾧ γὰρ μέτρῳ μετρεῖτε ἀντιμετρηθήσεται ὑμῖν).

2.2 Callixtus and the weeds

From the letter of Clement (at the end of the first century), with a jump of more than a century, we pass directly to the bishop Callixtus (who died in 222), who is a foundational figure in the development of the church of Rome.[15] The latter's posi-

---

[15] Between these two, the *Shepherd of Hermas*, datable to the middle of the second century, cannot be considered the direct expression of a presbyter since the author considers himself a prophet, even if his intent is to work in a way consonant with the presbyters and to preach to the entire church. In any case, we have in that work a complete absence of scriptural citations or allusions and thus not even a hint of the words of Jesus. While *Agape* is one of the virtues that are personified in the work, its place in the work is quite limited with respect to the centrality it has in Jesus's own words in the Gospel. See the remarks by M. Simonetti, "Il *Pastore* di Erma," 197. A persuasive, recent examination of the *Shepherd* is provided by E. Castelli, "Dati storici e aspetti romanzeschi nelle prime due Visioni del *Pastore* di Erma"; Id., "Gli esordi alternativi del

tion on penance comes down to us from the most hostile source imaginable: the author of the *Elenchus* (IX.12.20–23) (for some time identified as Hippolytus of Rome[16]), who competed with Callixtus for the *episkopè*. In a sense, what he says about Callixtus should not be included within my exposition here, since we are including only official documents. Moreover, this is an indirect report, perhaps of a discourse given privately within the council of presbyters. It is important, nonetheless, because it manifests the official position which Rome will maintain concerning penance, namely, to avoid rigorism. If Callixtus's discourse, reported in the *Elenchus*, with its biblical citations and what follows from them were to correspond to what was basically communicated by him, it would confirm his shrewdness in constructing an argument founded entirely on Scripture.

Callixtus begins with the question from the Letter to the Romans: "Who are you to pass judgment on slaves of another?" (Rom 14:4). This letter of course enjoyed particular attention in Rome even from the time of the *Letter of Clement*. Paul's question, outside of its context, creates its own sense, namely, judgment is not proper to man. Callixtus then cites the Gospel parable of the weeds: "Let the weeds grow up with the grain" (cf. Mt 13:30). Jesus's explanation, according to the Gospel of Matthew, pushes back to the end of the world the division between the children of the Kingdom and the children of evil, thus offering a response to Paul's question, namely, that God alone, through the Son of Man, can judge.[17] In light of this explanation it is possible to interpret allegorically the story of Noah's ark as an image of the Church in the present age, one full of both pure and impure animals, representing the good and the sinners.

Callixtus, naturally, does not lack daring, focusing as he does on the allegorical interpretation of the animals (it is clear that if the Law can proclaim certain animals impure, it is because they first exist at all, and therefore they are saved by Noah) and leaving aside the fact that with respect to human beings, only the family of Noah are saved, they being evidently the only ones worth saving. Furthermore, Paul did not intend his question to refer to sinners, but rather to settle the issue of the coexistence, caused by different dietary practices. Paul intended to exhort the fervent faithful to overlook each other's cultural differences and

---

Pastore di Erma." For an innovative vision of Herma's narrative, see A.K. Harkins, "Entering the Narrative World of Hermas's Visions."

16 Some scholars continue to identify this author with Hippolytus of Rome († 236). For the status quaestionis, see E. Norelli, *Il corpus attribuito a Ippolito*, in C. Moreschini - E. Norelli, *Storia della letteratura cristiana antica greca e latina. I: Da Paolo all'età costantiniana*. New revised and expanded edition, Morcelliana, Brescia 2019, pp. 432–484.

17 On the interpretation of the parable of the weeds up to the contemporary age see G. Ruggieri, *La zizzania nella chiesa e nel mondo*.

subgroup identities in the name of common faith in Jesus Christ.[18] Callixtus, on the other hand, bends Paul's exclamation toward the proper attitude to take toward sinners.[19] If Paul had actually faced sinners like those Callixtus refers to, it is legitimate to doubt that he would have been as indulgent, at least if we consider what he writes in 1 Cor 6 concerning lawsuits among believers and the instruction in 1 Cor 5:13 ("God will judge those outside. Drive out the wicked person from among you"). Callixtus strengthens Paul's rhetorical question arguing that only God and his Christ can give a decision to separate the sinner. (The theme of judgment was also present in Rom 14:10—a little later, but with a different meaning, calling to mind the equality of all before the divine βῆμα of judgment: "Why do you pass judgment on your brother or sister? Or you, why do you despise your brother or sister? For we will all stand before the judgment seat of God.") Reference to the Last Judgment of God will remain constant in the post-Constantinian bishops of Rome, but it is the frame of reference that changes.

According to Callixtus, the Church cannot but assume a posture of mercy because it is not the seat of judgment—only God can judge. Later bishops instead use the judgment of God to seal their own directives, which anticipate the judgment of God himself.

2.3 Stephen and the strange interpretation of Mt 16:18–19

The explosion of the question of baptism, a consequence of the Novatianist rigorist schism, reproduces the same layout we observed in the case of Callixtus, with the bishop lining up in favor of the validity of one baptism—in other words, in favor of a position considered as "lax" by the opponents. Here we have to point out perhaps the greatest loss of documentation from Roman sources in the pre-Constantine period, namely, the letters written by Stephen (bishop from 254 to 257) during the course of the polemic. From the pejorative words we have from Cyprian and Firmilian, all that comes to us is his extremely authoritarian attitude. Why is the lack of letters from Stephen himself so important? Because it keeps us from seeing the doctrinal and exegetical warrants of the Roman position with regard to the impossibility of rebaptizing those who received this Sacrament in heretical circles, that is, why the baptism was considered valid.

---

18 Cf. P.F. Esler, *Conflict and Identity in Romans. The Social Setting of Paul's Letter*, 339–356.
19 The verse of Paul was, in fact, used—as we see in the testimony of Tertullian (*De pudicitia* 2.2)—openly by those who desired to excuse the behavior of the faithful whom the rigorists, like Tertullian, considered laxists unworthy, particularly with reference to second marriages.

2.3 Stephen and the strange interpretation of Mt 16:18–19

It would seem that Stephen relies on a theology of the name, that is, on the power of the name of Christ. And this he does in continuity with the ultimate appeal to God in the line of Callixtus and the Jewish roots of Roman Christianity. On the other hand, this vision which would seem to place Christ ahead of the decision of the Church is also brought forward on the basis—this time explicitly—of a particularity of the Roman Church. From Firmilian we know that Stephen invoked an interpretation of the words attributed to Jesus in Mt 16:18–19 ("And I tell you, you are Peter, and on this rock I will build my church, and the gates of Hades will not prevail against it. I will give you the keys of the kingdom of heaven, and whatever you bind on earth will be bound in heaven, and whatever you loose on earth will be loosed in heaven"), which has no parallel in any sources outside of Rome and which will remain a characteristic of the Roman Church's position.[20] In Rome, one obeys and that is the final word. This seemingly comes from Stephen:

Firmilian, *ep.* 75, 17 (CSEL 3/2, 821,14–18. 25–26):

Atque ego in hac parte iuste indignor ad hanc tam apertam et manifestam Stephani stultitiam, quod qui sic de episcopatus sui loco gloriatur et se successionem Petri tenere contendit, super quem fundamenta ecclesiae collocata sunt, multas alias petras inducat et ecclesiarum multarum noua aedificia constituat [. . .] Stephanus qui per successionem cathedram Petri habere se praedicat.

At this point I become filled with righteous indignation at Stephen's crass and obvious stupidity. He is a man who finds the location of his bishopric such a source of pride, who keeps insisting that he occupies the succession to Peter, upon whom the foundations of the Church were laid; and yet, by using his authority to defend heretical baptism, he is introducing

---

20 Different interpretations of the passage from Matthew have developed in the third century. One possible interpretation identifies the rock with Peter. Tertullian however (*De pudicitia* 21,9–10), in his rigorist phase, denies that Peter's power can be transmitted to anyone. According to Cyprian of Carthage (*ep.* 33.1; *ep.* 66.8), Peter's prerogative is transmitted to all bishops, through succession. Another interpretation identifies the rock with Christ. Origen says (*In Mt.* XII,10.14) that every Christian becomes Peter if he, like Peter, recognizes Christ and imitates him. Consequently, every Christian has the power to bind and loose. Eastern patristics follows Origen. Augustine (*Sermo* 149,6.7) says that Peter symbolizes the Church. Luther and all the reformers followed Augustine: see E. Prinzivalli, "La componente patristica." It is interesting to note how Klaus Schatz, Jesuit and professor emeritus of Church history, in a volume (*Die päpstliche Primat*, Engl. transl. *Papal Primacy*) that is a classic in the Catholic rethinking of primacy on a more dialogic basis, recognizes that "if one had asked a Christian in the year 100, 200, or even 300 whether the bishop of Rome was the head of all Christians, or whether there was a supreme bishop over all the other bishops and having the last word in questions affecting the whole Church, he or she would certainly have said no" (*Papal Primacy*, 3).

many other rocks and he is laying the foundations of and building up many new churches [. . .] Stephen, who vaunts that he has succeeded to the occupancy of the chair of Peter.[21]

The immediate outcome of this position was that nothing came of it and Stephen's authoritarian *modus operandi* was ignored by his successors. Stephen took advantage of the appeal that was made to the Church of Rome. This circumstance was exploited by him and his successors (in similar cases) to affirm the rights and privileges of the Church of Rome and its concern and care for the whole Church (according to the language used at the time).

Stephen was succeeded by Sixtus the Second (257–258), who is immediately martyred, and then by Dionysius, from whom we have fragments of a letter to Dionysius of Alexandria (which we treated above), but given that this is more properly considered theological material, it is outside of our present scope.

Between Dionysius of Rome (259–267) and Julius the First (337–352), there is a vast lacuna of documentation: almost seventy years of silence from the nine bishops of Rome, in the period including Felix the First, Eutychian, Gaius, Marcellinus, Marcellus the First, Eusebius, Miltiades, Silvester, and Mark—from whom we have not one writing, not even a line.

---

21 English translation: G.W. Clarke: *The Letters of St. Cyprian of Carthage*, 88–89.

3 After Constantine: a summary table

Moving from Julius the First (337–352) to Boniface the First (418–422) includes a group of bishops in between: Liberius (352–366), Damasus (366–384), Siricius (384–398), Anastasius (399–402), Innocent the First (402–417), Zosimus (417–418). All of these reigned during the period of the consolidation of imperial Christianity as well as the greatest controversies.

At this point, given that the sources become abundant, it is interesting to look at some of the quantitative elements of our inquiry since, as we know, quantity becomes quality. I base myself here on a collection of data taken from the volumes of Hermann-Josef Sieben's *Vetustissimae epistulae Romanorum pontificum* (FC 58, 3 vols). I do not deny that the choice to rely on Sieben (but this would apply to any other editor) implies a certain amount of arbitrariness, because, especially in the case of possible biblical allusions, there is a margin of subjectivity in evaluating the possible allusion. With regard to Julius's letters, this subjectivity is proven by comparison with G.L. Thompson's edition,[22] which records a greater number of biblical allusions.[23] But, all things considered, even if we accept

---

[22] G.L. Thompson, *The Correspondence of Pope Julius I, Greek and Latin Text and English Translation with Introduction and Commentary*.

[23] The margin of subjectivity depends on the fact that the language of ecclesiastical authors is strongly imbued with biblicalisms. Hence, in my opinion, only those passages or terms where the author seems to *consciously* refer to a biblical verse should be reported as biblical allusions. Thompson notes in Julius's Letter to the Bishops assembled in Antioch (*ep.* 2, G.L Thompson, *The Correspondence*, 88–129) 15 allusions (2 Cor 11:13–15; 1 Cor 6:1–6; 1 Cor 14:12; 2 Cor 10:8. 13:10; Rom 6:17; 1 Cor 11:23; Num 15:30; Dt 9:18,22; Mal 2:17; 4 Mk 18:24; Gal 1:5; Phil 4:20; 2 Tm 4:18; Heb 13:21) and 2 quotations (Mt 16:16; Col 3:12) not reported by Sieben, while Sieben notes three allusions (1 Tm 1:10; 1 Cor 5:4; Jn 14:27) not reported by Thompson. Here, I cannot examine each case. I limit myself to a few observations. The quotation from Mt 16:16 noted by Thompson is certainly to be accepted (Σὺ εἶ ὁ Χριστὸς ὁ υἱὸς τοῦ θεοῦ τοῦ ζῶντος). In fact, Julius says (*ep.* 1,23,1, Sieben I, 96,11, cf. G.L Thompson, *The Correspondence*, 44,94): οὐδὲ εἰς ἄνθρωπον ἦσαν ἁμαρτήσαντες, ἀλλ' εἰς αὐτὸν τὸν κύριον ἡμῶν Ἰησοῦν Χριστὸν τὸν υἱὸν τοῦ θεοῦ τοῦ ζῶντος. The quotation, noted by Thompson, of the expression σπλάγχνα οἰκτιρμοῦ in Col 3:12 must also be accepted, since Julius says (*ep.* 1,34,3, Sieben I, 124,3; cf. G.L Thompson, *The Correspondence*, 76,452): σπουδάσατε ὡς σπλάγχνα ἔχοντες οἰκτιρμοῦ διορθώσασθαι. In both cases these are characteristic expressions of NT texts. The case of allusions is more complex, as I said above. For example, the final doxology of Julius's letter for which Thompson lists many allusions in combination (4 Mk 18:24; Gal 1:5; Phil 4:20; 2 Tm 4:18; Heb 13:21) was so usual that it was not connected to the afore mentioned biblical passages in the writer's mind. Conversely, at least one of the allusions reported by Sieben and not by Thompson is very important. It is Jn 14:27: Εἰρήνην ἀφίημι ὑμῖν, εἰρήνην τὴν ἐμὴν δίδωμι ὑμῖν. Julius consciously echoes it when he says (*ep.* 1,32,4, Sieben I, 120,6): αἱ δὲ ἐκκλησίαι εἰρήνην ἔχωσι πρὸς τὸ τὴν τοῦ κυρίου εἰρήνην τὴν δοθεῖσαν ἡμῖν.

Thompson's assessment, the relationships established on the basis of Sieben's edition do not change. Basing my evaluation on Sieben's work, I have produced the following summary in table form (Table 2).

Table 2: Summary of biblical quotations in early bishops of Rome (337–422).

Number of letters of the bishops	Total biblical quotations or allusions	Gospels' quotations or allusions[24]	Pauline letters' quotations or allusions	Other New Testament writings' quotations or allusions	Old Testament's quotations or allusions
Julius I = 2	10	3 (3)	7	0	0
Liberius = 12	9	1 (0)	6	0	2
Damasus = 12	106	37 (8)	32	5	32
Siricius = 5	50	8 (8)	25	4	13
Anastasius = 3	3	0	2	0	1
Innocent I = 36	75	10 (7)	32	8	25
Zosimus = 16	25	6 (4)	6	3	10
Boniface I = 10	15	9 (7)	3	2	1

In the table, all of the letters that we have from these Roman bishops are taken into account. Some of the letters, of course, are addressed to individuals and they show the characteristics of a practical rather than an official discourse. It is precisely these letters that generally lack biblical quotations. I say "generally" because there are of course exceptions: for example, the letters of Damasus to Jerome turn on scriptural issues and so naturally have citations. In fact, Damasus has a much greater number of citations and allusions than any of the other bishops. We can explain this, in part, from the interest in Scripture that Damasus manifests in his career. But the principal motive is given by the fact that the *Decretum Damasi* has a whole series of the titles of Jesus drawn from the Scriptures (the *epinoiai* according to Origen), accounting for 46 of his citations and allusions. Also, we should recognize that official letters are usually addressed to councils of bishops or other groups of bishops. Nevertheless, even in the case of a specialized, "internal" vocabulary, the use of particular words instead of others is not any less significant.

Now we can analyze the numbers found in the table, which without an explanation are possibly misleading. What jumps out to the eye is that two of the bishops (Liberius and Anastasius) manifest no citations of the words of Jesus.

---

24 In parentheses the actual quotations or allusions to the *logia* of Jesus.

4 The silence of Anastasius and Liberius

In the case of Anastasius, one can explain the lack of quotations of Jesus from the fact that we have only a small number of his letters preserved, and all of those are about a circumscribed topic (they all deal with the Origenist question)—but that only partially explains it. The rather superficial way in which Anastasius confronts the accusations against Origen and Rufinus does not testify in favor of a particularly intellectual stature for this bishop, whom Jerome praised shamelessly precisely for his position against Origen. It is true that we cannot judge the scriptural culture of the three citations we have, all the more since the bishops enjoyed the use of some assistance in the editing of their letters. Nonetheless, we have to recognize that none of them allow us to detect that he took any pains to strengthen his discourse with the Bible. One citation is a simple form of anathema (Gal 1:8); another is Paul's introductory praise of the Romans in the letter addressed to them, which Anastasius cites for his interlocutor, Venerius of Milan, in a way that is inclusive of all;[25] and the last, which seems the most specific, is taken from 1 Sam 16:7 and refers to the famous episode where God chooses David.

It is likewise interesting to note the absence of the words of Jesus in Liberius, in the context of an overall lack of references to Scripture whatsoever. He was surely a pious man. We know of his travails during the Arian crisis, his strenuous defense of Athanasius and the Nicene Creed, his exile and subsequent recanting, his return to Rome, and the support of his people. Nevertheless, the rarity of scriptural references and the absence of the words of Jesus are difficult to justify given the topics he discussed. If one wants to be guided by a meditation on Scripture and the Gospel, then any occasion is a good one. It is true that we can observe an indirect allusion (not noted by Sieben and which therefore I have not included in the table) to the context of Mt 16:18–19, when, at the beginning of the letter to Eusebius of Vercelli, Liberius praises the interlocutor because, he says, "by following the teachings of the gospel, you have not moved away in any way from unity with the Apostolic See" (*secutus euangeliorum praecepta nullo genere a consortio sedis apostolicae discrepasti*).[26] But in this case we are in the usual sphere of defense of the prerogatives of the Roman See. Thus, our wonder is justified, above all considering the fact that, as an enthusiastic epitaph records, as Liberius went through the *cursus honorum*, he was at one time a *lector scripturarum* (ICUR, n.s. IX, n. 24830).

---

25 Cf. E. Prinzivalli, "Anastasio I di Roma e le lettere ai vescovi di Milano sulla condanna di Origene," 25.
26 Liberius, *ep.* 2, Sieben I, 142,2–3.

5 Julius the First and the Roman *agape*

Let us concentrate now on the cases in which the citations of Scripture either abound or at least are present in a significant amount in order to see what role is played by the *logia* of Jesus (which I defined at the beginning). Looking at the numbers, largely speaking the citations or allusions to the *logia* of Jesus are a small minority compared to the citations of Old Testament texts, but especially compared to the Pauline letters. This, at least, is obvious: given that the majority of the letters deal with disciplinary issues and, to some degree, theological controversies, it is clear that the letters of the Pauline corpus, especially the Pastoral Letters, prevail insofar as they contain both disciplinary reflection as well as theological material.

From Julius the First on, the bishops of Rome place greater and greater decided emphasis on their authority as the last instance of judgment, notwithstanding the ascent of a Christian emperor—the exception being during the reign of Julian the Apostate—which establishes a competing point of reference. Julius the First (337–352), the predecessor of Liberius, himself was involved in the Arian controversy and he established the posture continued by his successors. From Julius we have an important and long letter, written to the Eastern bishops in the summer of 341, during the full swing of the Arian controversy, which seeks to rehabilitate Athanasius of Alexandria and Marcellus of Ancyra. Julius dwells at length on refuting the disciplinary accusation against Athanasius and argues against the canonical validity of the Council of Tyre (335), while dedicating only a few lines to the doctrinal accusation made by the Eusebians against Marcellus. Julius limits himself to accepting the affirmations by Marcellus: "Concerning our Lord and Savior Jesus Christ, he confessed that he holds the same pious beliefs as the Catholic Church."[27] What is interesting is to see his use of the words of Jesus. Julius knows that at the center of Jesus's message is *agape*. In fact, he begins by declaring in an absolutely programmatic manner that he had written to the Easterners with love and understanding. They, however, responded with a spirit of dispute, which is contrary to faith in Christ.[28]

---

[27] G.L. Thompson (ed.), *The Correspondence of Pope Julius I, ep.* II, 70,380–381 and trans., 71: οὕτως γὰρ εὐσεβῶς περὶ τοῦ κυρίου καὶ σωτῆρος ἡμῶν Ἰησοῦ Χριστοῦ ὡμολόγησε φρονεῖν, ὥσπερ καὶ ἡ καθολικὴ ἐκκλησία φρονεῖ.

[28] Cf. *Ibidem*, 38, 6–9: ἡμεῖς μὲν ἀγάπῃ καὶ συνειδήσει ἀληθείας ἐγράψαμεν, ὑμεῖς δὲ μετὰ φιλονεικίας, καὶ οὐχ ὡς ἔπρεπεν, ἐπεστείλατε [. . .] ταῦτα δὲ ἀλλότρια τῆς ἐν Χριστῷ πίστεώς ἐστιν.

Julius's lament returns over and over again, even to the point of desolation at the end: "My beloved, church decisions are no longer made according to the gospel, but with a view to banishment and death."[29] Even if these are not the words of Jesus on love, the programmatic aspect of mutual love enters into the discourse in order to signal the difference between himself and his interlocutors. Thus, it comes as a sort of vindication and accusation. From this point of view, Julius's letter is for us the first example of the rhetorical practice which was constantly adopted by the bishops of Rome. Whenever a bishop of Rome refers to love and peace—with an allusion to the passage in Jn 14:27 ("Peace I leave with you; my peace I give to you"), which returns in Siricius (in the letter to the African bishops) and in Innocent the First (to Anysius of Thessalonica)—he takes for himself, in a programmatic way, the Gospel practice in order to admonish his interlocutor.

---

[29] Cf. *Ibidem*, 78,485–486 and trans., 79: ὦ ἀγαπητοί, οὐκέτι κατὰ τὸ εὐαγγέλιον, ἀλλὰ λοιπὸν ἐπὶ ἐξορισμῷ καὶ θανάτῳ αἱ κρίσεις τῆς ἐκκλησίας εἰσίν.

6 The typologies of the *logia* of Jesus quoted by the bishops

Let us look now, in a thematic manner, at the three typologies of the *logia* of Jesus quoted or alluded to by the bishops:

Admonition: Mt 18:6 ("If any of you cause one of these little ones who believe in me to sin, it would be better for you if a great millstone were fastened around your neck and you were drowned in the depth of the sea") by Julius;[30] Mk 7:9 (*Reiecistis mandatum Dei ut traditiones uestras statuatis*; "you have rejected God's precept to establish your traditions") by Damasus (to the Gauls)[31] and Siricius to the Italian bishops;[32] Lk 12:48 (*Cui multum creditum fuerit, plus ab eodem requiretur*; "From everyone to whom much has been given, much will be required") by Siricius to the African bishops[33] and Innocent the First to Victricius of Rouen.[34] In general, Siricius makes broad use of these *logoi* of admonition—for example, Mt 7:15 (*Multi uenient ad uos in uestitu ouium, intus sunt lupi rapaces, a fructibus eorum cognoscetis eos*; "Many will come to you in sheep's clothing but inwardly are ravenous wolves! You will know them by their fruits") to the Italian bishops concerning the question of Jovinian.[35]

Threat: These are used above all at the end of letters, to reinforce the admonition. Thus, Julius the First reminds the Eastern bishops of the words of final judgment that come to everyone—Mt 12:36 ("I tell you, on the day of judgment you will have to give an account for every careless word you utter")[36]; or Mt 15:13 (*Omnis plantatio quam non plantauit Pater meus caelestis, eradicabitur*; "Every plant that my heavenly Father has not planted will be uprooted") by Damasus to Acolius.[37] Interesting also is the *agraphon* from Revelation 22:12 which Siricius (Letter to the bishops of Africa) uses only in the final part: *custodiet Dominus cor-*

---

[30] Julius, *ep*. 1, Sieben I, 90,25–27; after the period I have considered: pope Celestine I, *ep*. 2, Sieben III, 810, and *ep*. 15,856.
[31] Damasus, *Ad Gallos*, 2, Sieben I, 240,73.
[32] Siricius, *ep*. 3, Sieben II, 336,7.
[33] Siricius, *ep*. 2, Sieben II, 328,22.
[34] In this case it is an allusion: *Cui multum enim creditur, plus ab eo exigitur, usura poenarum*: Innocent I, *ep*. 2, Sieben II, 374,20–21.
[35] Innocent quotes freely, replacing the initial imperative (*Attendite uobis a falsis prophetis*) with the certainty of the advent of many: *ep*. 5, Sieben II, 346,5–6.
[36] Julius, *ep*. 1, Sieben I, 128,17.
[37] Damasus, *ep*. 8, Sieben I, 266,7–9. The verse will also be used by Celestine, *ep*. 15, Sieben III, 862, 10 and by Sixtus III, *ep*. 3, Sieben III, 892,13, in both cases in the form of an allusion.

pora nostra et animas nostras in diem qua "redditurus est unicuique secundum opera sua" ("The Lord will preserve our bodies and our souls until the day he repays according to everyone's work").[38]

Supporting disciplinary instructions: The *logia* which stand out here are the ones that prohibit divorce and those that promote continence. For example, Mt 19:11 (*Non omnes capiunt uerbum* Dei, *sed his qui datum est*; "Not everyone can receive this saying of God, but those to whom it is given") in Damasus's letter to the bishops of Gaul, where he—probably intentionally—substitutes the various translations of "this saying" (*verbum istud, hoc verbum, verbum hoc*) with *verbum Dei*.[39] Also Mt 19:6 (*quod deus iunxit, homo non separet*; "What God has joined together, let not man separate")[40] and Mt 19:9 (*Qui dimiserit uxorem suam, et duxerit aliam, moechatur; similiter et qui dimissam duxerit, moechatur*; "Anyone who repudiates his wife and marries another commits adultery; just as he who marries the repudiated woman commits adultery") by Innocent the First.[41]

---

[38] Siricius, *ep.* 2, Sieben II, 334,16.
[39] Damasus, *Ad Gallos*, 12, Sieben I, 254,17–18. Y.-M. Duval, *La décrétale* Ad Gallos episcopos, 102, notes that Jerome has the same expression *verbum Dei* in his letter to Eustochius (*ep.* 22,19).
[40] Innocent I, ep. 4, Sieben II, 402,11–12 and Innocent I, *ep.* 13, Sieben II, 446, 14–15. According to Sieben, Innocent here quotes Mk 10:9, but in reality it is always Mt 19:6, because in the Vetus Mk predominantly has the verb *disiungat* (see P. Sabatier III, 223).
[41] Innocent I, *ep.* 5, Sieben II, 412,15–16.

7 From Damasus to Siricius: the perfecting of the decretal letters

7.1 Damasus and the *Ad Gallos*

Disciplinary instruction is a privileged part of the so-called "decretals," and thus we should say a word about them. The first decretal letter that has come down to us is the *Ad Gallos* of Damasus. The manuscripts do not give the name of the bishop to whom it is addressed. It has been variously attributed (to Siricius or to Innocent the First), but in 1904 Babut[42] advanced the name of Damasus, which was confirmed by the series of convincing arguments given by Y.-M. Duval in 2005,[43] who went so far as to individuate the hand of Jerome in the letter and thus date it to the years 383–384.

But what is a decretal? In the history of the Church, documents coming from the popes that had a general character and which were redacted in the form of a letter were called "decretals" or "decretal letters." These often contained juridical norms and had the force of law for all the faithful, unless they were written with reference to particular laws or cases, in which case they were addressed to determinate regions or persons. With Damasus—if the *Ad Gallos* is in fact his—the Church of Rome expresses, for the first time (to our knowledge), judgments and disciplinary instructions from the pope's authority using this expression, modelled after the language and manner of the rescripts that came out of the imperial bureaucracy. The *ratio* which Duval recognizes in the author of the decretal is the justification of his decisions by arguing in part from Scripture but first and foremost to argue "par la raison".[44] I would add, however, that all of this presupposes the authority of the *Sedes apostolica*.

The prologue of the letter, which has come down very poorly to us in the manuscript tradition, is the most important part. The first word of the letter is *Dominus*, in reference to Christ, and the evangelical invocation is obvious. What stands out as the *leitmotiv* is the intertwining of the words taken from Mt 7:7 and Lk 11:9 (*Petite et <accipietis>*;[45] *quaerite et inuenietis; pulsate et aperietur uobis*; "Ask and you shall receive; seek and you will find; knock and it will be opened to

---

[42] Cf. E. Ch. Babut, *La plus ancien décrétale*.
[43] Cf. Y.-M. Duval, *La décrétale* Ad Gallos episcopos: *son texte et son auteur*.
[44] *Ibidem*, Avant-propos, viii.
[45] Duval rightly (*La décrétale* Ad Gallos episcopos, 55) prefers the lesson of MS *Stuttgart, Württembergische Landesbibliothek*, HB VI 113, ff. 79–81 (s. VIII–IX) which preserves the Vetus (*accipietis*), instead of the Vulgate (*dabitur uobis*).

you") and Mt 7:8 and Lk 11:10 (*Omnis enim qui petit accipit, et qui quaerit inuenit et pulsanti aperitur*; "For everyone who asks receives, he who seeks finds, and to the one knocking it will be opened"), which Damasus uses to exhort the seeker of truth not to "set out after empty things" but to be "anxious at work" (*non inani profectu, sed labore[s] sollicit[ud]o*).⁴⁶ These biblical quotes (Mt 7:7-8; Lk 11:9-10) were widely used by the Gnostics. They were, then, in circulation in the Alexandrian tradition, in response to the Gnostics claims; therefore, these verses also found their way into the works of Ambrose and Jerome, thus confirming the influence of Jerome. Whereas the exhortation to knock and ask came from Christ himself, the requested response, however, comes rather from the bishop of Rome (*Vnde eadem repetere mihi quidem non est molestum: uobis enim necessarium est*; "Therefore, to repeat these same things is not an annoyance to me: but it is necessary for you"). In consequence, the argument then turns immediately to the *auctoritas sedis apostolicae* (I.2), which must ask in regards both to the *legis scientia* as well as to the *traditiones* (here, he means the "apostolic" traditions) whence comes the praise to the Gauls who have demanded such from the Apostolic See, while many bishops, with worldly presumption, change the traditions, when "the Scriptures" (i.e. Jesus) say: (*scriptura diuina dicente*) *Reiecistis mandatum Dei, ut traditiones uestras statuatis* ("you have rejected the commandment of God to observe your traditions"; cf. Mk 7:9).

The majority of the *Ad Gallos* takes up the discipline of chastity. In particular, it tackles the questions surrounding the consecrated virgins who have fallen, either before or after their veiling, and the penance to which they are subject; the chastity of clerics, even if they are married; and the behaviors which disqualify a man for priestly ordination. As to the context in which the "Golden Rule" is invoked, I will return to that later.

7.2 Siricius and the decretal to Himerius

The decretal of Damasus's successor Siricius to Himerius of Tarragona (385) is one of the most important decretals and it is included in all the most ancient collections. Notwithstanding the similarities of content between the two decretals, the atmosphere of the second is different. "È scritta in tono fermo e veramente romano" ("It is written in a tone both firm and truly Roman").⁴⁷ Here, the modali-

---

46 Damasus, *Ad Gallos, exordium*, Y.-M. Duval, *La décrétale* Ad Gallos episcopos, 24 and *apparatus*.
47 F. Di Capua, "Da Siricio a Sisto III," 146.

ties of the Roman imperial chancery are already fully employed. The analogy between the series of imperial and papal documents does not end at the fact that the origin of canon law dates back to the collections of decretals and to the extracts from the conciliar canons, just as the *Codex* of Theodosius was made up of the legislative passages taken from the imperial constitutions. For even the external form of these works are similar in that both are composed in a rhythmic literary style.

While the prologue to the letter to the Gauls was marked by the words of Christ which were assumed to refer to the teaching authority of the Church of Rome, with Siricius the presumption is completely based on his own personal authority that comes from his status as the successor to Damasus, to whom Himerius had addressed his letter. Also, with Siricius the words of Jesus function as reinforcements for disciplinary instructions. In reference to the reconciliation of apostates, for whom reconciliation can only come at the point of death, Siricius writes that they are to be accepted, and he echoes what he says are the words of Jesus (the expression *docente Domino* is without a doubt a reference to Christ), which are in fact those of Ezekiel (18:23) about not wanting the death of the sinner but that he be converted and lives. In this case the phrase corresponds to the evangelical spirit which is understood clearly to be the same as a saying of Jesus. The severity of the laws on priestly continence are reinforced with the mention of the instructions of Moses for the priests of the Temple, and for this purpose Siricius uses Mt 5:17, where Jesus says that he came to fulfill the Law not to solve it: *unde et Dominus Iesus cum nos suo illustrasset aduentu, in Euangelio protestatur, quia Legem uenerit impleret, non soluere* ("Thus, the Lord Jesus shows us in his coming, as the Gospel insists, to fulfill the Law not to abolish it").[48]

In the course of the letter (n. 3), Siricius recalls the words of Jesus in Mt 16:18, which we saw were used by the Church of Rome with confidence from the time of Stephen (and probably even before) and which had acquired with Damasus a programmatic meaning. Mt 16:18–19 in fact appears in a major way in the so-called *Decretum Damasi*,[49] appended to the council at Rome in 382. That letter deals with the response from Rome to the anti-Roman spirit of the third canon of the Council of Constantinople in 381. Mt 16:18–19 is interpreted in a juridical and disciplinary spirit, as is enunciated clearly:

---

[48] Siricius, *ep.* 1,10, Sieben II, 316,2–3.
[49] The third of five chapters of a composite document that has been known since the seventh century as the *Decretum de libris recipiendis et non recipiendis*, traditionally attributed to Pope Gelasius and for this reason also known as the *Decretum Gelasianum*. See U. Reutter, *Damasus, Bischof von Rom (366–384)*, 468–513.

III. Post has omnes propheticas et euangelicas atque apostolicas quas superius deprompsimus scripturas, quibus ecclesia catholica per gratiam Dei fundata est, etiam illud intimandum putauimus quod, quamuis uniuersae per orbem catholicae diffusae ecclesiae, unus thalamus Christi sit, sancta tamen Romana ecclesia nullis synodicis constitutis ceteris ecclesiis praelata est, sed euangelica uoce domini et saluatoris nostri primatum obtenuit: "tu es Petrus inquiens —et super hanc petram aedificabo ecclesiam meam et portae inferni non praeualebunt aduersus eam; et tibi dabo claues regni caelorum, et quaecumque ligaueris super terram erunt ligata et in caelo, et quaecumque solueris super terram erunt soluta et in coelo."[50]

After all these prophetic and evangelical and apostolic writings which we have quoted above, upon which the Catholic Church is founded by the grace of God, we believe it must also be pointed out that, though the Catholic Church is scattered throughout the world, there is a single bridal chamber of Christ. So, the Holy Roman Church is not preferred to the other Churches by any decisions of the synods, but has been given precedence by the evangelical voice of our Lord and Redeemer, who says: "you are Peter, and on this rock I will build my church, and the gates of Hades will not prevail against it. I will give you the keys of the kingdom of heaven, and whatever you bind on earth will be bound in heaven, and whatever you loose on earth will be loosed in heaven."

---

50 *Decretum Damasi* III.1, Sieben I, 276–278.

8 The paradoxes of Innocent and Zosimus

In his many letter and decretals, Innocent the First dedicates much space to respond to questions about marriage, connected more or less to the dignity of the priesthood. In his letter to the Synod of Toledo in 404,[51] Innocent calls to mind the words of Jesus on marriage in Mt 19:6 (*quod Deus iunxit, homo non separet*). In his letter to Exsuperius,[52] where he engages the problem of marriage and adultery, he recalls Mt 19:9 (*Qui dimiserit uxorem suam et duxerit aliam, moechatur; similiter et qui dimissam duxerit, moechatur*). He argues similarly on the same point with Rufus with reference to the scam wherein *clerici* took another wife after baptism, under the pretext of considering the first marriage abrogated. In contrast, the pope quotes Mt 19:6 (*Quod ergo Deus iunxerit, homo non separet*; "Because what God has joined, let no man separate").[53] The clerics, to circumvent the canonical prohibition on remarrying in the event of widowhood, appealed to the circumstance of having lost their wives when they were catechumens: therefore, baptism constituted them new men, and from this condition derived the lawfulness of marrying again. Innocent counterargues, not without irony, that baptism washes away sins: therefore, let us say whether marriage is or is not a sin. If it is, the creator of the sin is the one who commanded the union between man and woman (i.e. God), if it is not, then it is a command of good and baptism does not eliminate the good. It is interesting to note how Innocent, citing Matthew, systematically leaves out the exception clause (Mt 5:32; Mt 19:9)—it cannot be a coincidence that he interprets Matthew in agreement with the other two Synoptics, as Augustine did at the same time.[54]

Having come to this point, perhaps you are asking yourselves if and how often the commandment to love, in the various forms it takes in the Gospels, is cited. As to the love of one's enemies (Mt 5:44 and Lk 6:27), it is never spoken of. This can be explained in part by the fact that we are speaking of speeches and letters which are internal to the Christian churches, where it is assumed that one speaks to one's companions in the Faith. But it can also be explained by the objective difficulty of this commandment, which is not by chance that it finds itself in an ambivalent situation; on the one hand it is passed over, or attenuated by Christian exegetes, as it is the case in the *Didache*, on the other hand it is understood

---

51 Cf. *supra*, note 40.
52 Cf. *supra*, note 41.
53 Innocent I, *ep.* 13,5, Sieben II, 446,14–15.
54 Cf. Augustin, *De coniugiis adulterinis* 1.8.8–10.11.

as an absolutely distinctive element of Christians.⁵⁵ Damasus (to the bishops of Gaul) presents the Golden Rule in its Gospel form from Mt 7:12 (*quae enim uultis ut faciant uobis homines, eadem et uobis facite illis*; "what you want men to do for you, do you the same to them").⁵⁶ Here, we are in a specific context: the pope imposes the rule that a cleric condemned by the bishop of a certain church cannot be received in another.⁵⁷ Thus, the rule serves to reinforce the instruction for reciprocity with respect to bishops.

The sole bishop to cite the commandment of love to one's neighbor, right at the moment of the clash of the African bishops, is Zosimus. His case merits attention. As we know, Zosimus has passed into history as the bishop who, while demonstrating an active spirit in the two short years of his reign, did not succeed in achieving any of his goals.⁵⁸ On the Pelagian question, after having sought to rehabilitate Pelagius and (with some differences) Caelestius, he was constrained by the pincer move of the African bishops and the Emperor Honorius to change his position and issue his *Tractoria*. We cannot here even touch lightly on this complicated set of events. What I can do is make two rather easily agreed-upon observations:

1. This incident which involved Pelagius carried with it, with the backing of Augustine's powerful reflection, a development: we passed from a general and shared notion of Grace to a previously unknown definition of its nature and manner of action.⁵⁹

---

55 The author of *Didache* (I,2) writes at first: προσεύχεσθε ὑπὲρ τῶν ἐχθρῶν ὑμῶν ("pray for your enemies") and immediately after: Ὑμεῖς δὲ φιλεῖτε τοὺς μισοῦντας ὑμᾶς καὶ οὐχ ἕξετε ἐχθρόν ("But love those who hate you, and you shall not have an enemy"). The first sentence modifies the saying of Mt 5:44 and Lk 6:27, which both have the verb form: ἀγαπᾶτε. It is not at all certain that the author of the *Didache* knew Matthew, but it is nevertheless significant that his tradition attenuates the meaning of Jesus's words. Indeed, at first he encourages the listeners to pray for enemies, and, then, he uses the verb φιλέω, which is weaker than ἀγαπάω, by accompanying the exhortation with the certainty of a positive reciprocity, that is, not having enemies. On the contrary, Marcion considers the commandment of love toward enemies so distinctive of the message of Jesus as to distinguish the God of love from the vengeful God of the Old Testament: in contrast, Tertullian tries to show that Isaiah 66:5 (according to the Septuagint, not according to the Hebrew) has the same meaning, hence there is only one God (Tertullian, *Adversus Marcionem* IV. 16.1).
56 Damasus, *Ad Gallos*, 17, Sieben I, 260,13–14.
57 This topic, as Damasus recalls, had already been discussed in the synods. At Nicaea with the canons 15 and 16: see A. Weckwerth, "The Twenty Canons of the Council of Nicaea." See also Serdica, canon 11.
58 Cf. M. Marcos, "Papal Authority, Local Autonomy and Imperial Control," 145–166.
59 Cf. É. Rebillard, "Sociologie de la déviance et orthodoxie. Le cas de la controverse pélagienne sur la grâce," 231.

2. From the time of Damasus—who, despite approaching the matter from a Western perspective, had familiarized himself with the Arian controversy to the extent of refining some of his initial imprudent doctrinal statements[60] – the bishops of Rome no longer personally addressed doctrinal questions or offered their own explanations in the field of theology.

Innocent the First, presented with the requests of the Africans, proceeds down the path of disengagement. He is bound, on the basis of the dossier of the Africans, to favor their side, and validate the excommunication of Pelagius and Caelestius,[61] but at the same time, he is open to the possibility of an appeal coming to Rome. The motive for Innocent's two-fold approach is rooted in his conception, and the one shared by his predecessors, of the role of the bishop of Rome. If Rome represents the court of last appeal, this has to be true also for a repentant sinner. But the reception of his position was different between the two parties. The Africans considered the condemnation definitive, receiving only the first part of Innocent's position. Pelagius and Caelestius, however, presenting themselves to Rome (Caelestius in person, Pelagius with a letter) relied on the second part which allowed for the possibility of an appeal. Innocent, taking everything into consideration, considered them certainly guilty, on the basis of the dossier which the Africans had prepared with a carefully designed strategy: in the end, to corroborate their own position which drew not a little criticism. Vice versa, the two, who considered themselves unjustly condemned, saw in the possibility offered by Innocent the occasion to show themselves beyond accusation.

For the rest, Innocent's responses to the African bishops would have surely been approved by Caelestius and Pelagius, insofar as they did not in any way distance themselves from the common position on the relationship between grace and prayer. In a difficult situation created by his predecessor, Zosimus sought to evaluate the situation on his own.[62] In the first place, we should note that with regard to his African interlocutors the pope makes use of the symbouleutic genre which characterized, centuries before, the letter of Clement to the Corinthians (it was not by chance that Caelestius happened to be summoned to the church of Saint Clement), distancing himself as he did both from the tone of his previous letters as well as those of his predecessors. In other words, the pope seeks to convince more than to deliberate, perhaps recognizing that he could not have forced

---

60 See U. Reutter, *Damasus, Bischof von Rom (366–384)*, 200–204.
61 Cf. M. Lamberigts, "Was Innocent Familiar with the Content of the Pelagian Controversy?," 203–223.
62 Cf. E. Prinzivalli, "Amate pacem, diligite caritatem, studete concordiam. Quando il papa sbaglia: Celestio e Pelagio tra Innocenzo I e Zosimo," 51–88.

anyone's hand at all. In any case, whether Zosimus's approach is seen as utilitarian or sincere, the objective fact remains that in these two letters the Gospel theme of mutual love resonates more than in all those of the predecessors, even apart from the small number of Gospel citations. Already in the introduction of the letter to Caelestius, Zosimus uses a citation of 1 Jn 4:8, which, even if it is not a *logion* of Jesus, identifies God with love. In the letter regarding Pelagius, he mentions the words of Jesus about the love of neighbor. In the first letter, there are no citations of Jesus, but there is nonetheless a constant call to love. At the end of the letter, he writes:

> 10. *caritatem uestram tam apostolicae sedis auctoritate quam mutua amoris affectione commoneo. Vtinam ingenia nostra sanctarum omnium scripturarum, quae secundum traditionem patrum atque maiorum receptae sunt, praeceptis obseruationibusque sufficiant! Quid illic non abundans, quid non dei spiritu et uocibus plenum sit? Nisi libet unumquemque plus sibi credere de se uti iudicio.*[63]

> I exhort your Charity both by the authority of the Apostolic See and by our mutual love. Ah, that our spirit should content itself with the prescriptions and instructions of the whole of Holy Scripture, which were received according to the tradition of the fathers and the ancestors! What is there not abounding, what is not full of the Spirit and Word of God? Unless someone likes to trust themselves more and build on their own judgment.

In the second letter (September 21, 417), the key words from before reappear—the search for peace, love, and concord:

> 8. *amate pacem, diligite charitatem, studete concordiam.*[64] *Nam scriptum est: diliges proximum tuum tamquam te ipsum. Qui magis alter alteri proximi sumus, quam omnes in Christo unum esse debemus?*[65]

> Love peace, choose love, strive for unity! Because it is written: "You shall love your neighbor as yourself" (Mt 19:19). But who is—one to the other—more "neighbor" than we, who are all to be one in Christ?

Zosimus does not enter into doctrinal argumentation. This absence—for which we can cite the illustrious precedent of Julius the First in the letter to the Eastern bishops in defense of Marcellus of Ancyra, but also the less illustrious Anastasius against Origen—could be read as a prolonging of a tendency toward disengagement on the doctrinal level which had characterized the substance of Innocent the First's writings as well. I think, however, that in this case we have to consider the

---

[63] Zosimus, *ep.* 2,10, Sieben II, 588.
[64] Di Capua, "Da Siricio a Sisto III (Le epistole di Zosimo)," 210, considers the letter written with true oratory enthusiasm, and some trispondaic cursus are noteworthy. *Contentio* often predominates with all the figures of this oratorical form.
[65] Zosimus, *ep.* 3,8, Sieben II, 596, 1–4.

possibility that Zosimus in fact rejected any content relating to the doctrinal dispute. He warned both Caelestius in particular and all *sacerdotes* in general in different places (thus, in all the places where the conflict developed) not to get involved in vain questions which derived from *curiositas* and which come from an excessive desire for dispute.[66] The final exhortation is significant, where Zosimus admonishes them to comply with the precepts of the Scriptures, according to the tradition of the Fathers. Naturally, it is easy to object that on the controversy at hand, the tradition either did not exist or at least was not unanimous, but precisely because of this absence of definition, one could plead that people not tear each other apart.[67]

As is well known, and as I have already said, the final result was catastrophic for Zosimus. It was proof of how different reality was from theory: the Petrine authority, at that time, mattered only insofar as it was in agreement with the requests of the episcopacies which turned to it for support. One of the paradoxes of this incident is to realize how Zosimus, while he sought to convince his interlocutors, did not exaggerate his Petrine authority. It was only when things were already turning for the worse, that in his harsh response to Aurelius he drew on the weapons of the Roman claims in his citation of Matthew 16:19.[68]

Zosimus's successor, Boniface the First, probably had the means of reflecting attentively on this incident. With him, for the first time, the number of citations of the words of Jesus surpass that of other biblical citations. But, if we look carefully, we see that, apart from the calming of the sea (thus, a miracle, not a word; Mt 14:28ff) and a reference to meekness of heart, there is only one citation of the words of Jesus, which is from Mt 16:18–19, that is always repeated in the hopes that it becomes an effective reality.

---

66 Zosimus, *ep.* 2,9, 588: *ipse sane Caelestius et quicumque in tempore ex diuersis regionibus aderant sacerdotes admoniti has tendiculas quaestionum et inepta certamina, quae non aedificant sed magis destruunt, ex illa curiositatis contagione profluere, dum unusquisque ingenio suo et intemperanti eloquentia supra scripta abutitur, cum in hoc etiam magnorum uirorum nonnumquam cum ipsis auctoribus scripta periclitantur post multam temporis miseriam interpretantis arbitrio, ut diuine profectum sit et multiloquio non euitari peccatum et sanctus Dauid merito postularet circumstantiam labiis suis orique custodiam.*—"I warned Celestius himself and all the priests, who from different regions were present at that moment, that these traps of questions and vain disputes, which do not edify but rather destroy, arise from the contagion of curiosity. Everyone misuses their intelligence and immoderate eloquence by despising Scripture, because even after a long time the writings of great men sometimes with their own authors are endangered by the arbitrariness of the interpreter: as God said, speaking too much becomes a sin (Prov 10:19) and David rightly asks for protection over his lips and a guard over his mouth (Ps 140:3)."
67 The times in which Origen was able to contemplate the possibility of open questions, in the prologue of his *De principiis*, had passed. Besides that, he had also paid the price, during his life, for the fact that the situation of the bishops was far removed from the schools of philosophy.
68 Cf. Zosimus, *ep.* 12,2, Sieben II, 634.

9 The homilies of Leo the Great

Let us now pass on to a comparison which presents elements of interest that both confirm and partially counterbalance what we have shown up until now. The first Roman homiletic corpus that has come down to us is that of Leo the First,[69] called "the Great." We could investigate endlessly the reason for the lack of homilies from his predecessors in a place like Rome where the supreme duty of preaching that falls on the bishop was proclaimed with such solemnity.[70] The witness of Leo the Great seems to contradict Sozomen's account, according to which in Rome neither the bishop nor others preached at all, unless the historian is merely speaking of an otherwise unknown and passing situation caused by the Arian crisis.[71] Yet even if the *institutio* of this bishop appears to have been decisively higher than normal, his preaching activity could not have come out of nowhere. If, as seems to be the case, there are no homilies preserved from his predecessors as bishops of Rome, this tells us that they were aware that their capacity for eloquence was modest (this of course could not be the case for Damasus) and thus it did not merit to be transmitted for posterity. Or, at least, they thought that this part of their activity was worthy of less attention than their other duties at the time (which is significant in itself).[72]

For Leo, this was not the case. He took the greatest care in the preparation of his sermons and in their revision for publication.[73] His preaching, collected in five cycles, presents a total of almost 100 homilies given over the space of 20 years. This is not a lot, given the long span of his pontificate, but their precise and

---

[69] In recent years there has been a flourishing of studies on Pope Leo I. I would like to point out the following studies: M.J. Armitage, *A Twofold Solidarity: Leo the Great's Theology of Redemption*; H. Feichtinger, *Die Gegenwart Christi in der Kirche bei Leo dem Grossen*; S. Wessel, *Leo the Great and the Spiritual Rebuilding of a Universal Rome*; L. Pidolle, *La christologie historique du pape saint Léon le Grand*. Historical and theological summaries: B. Green, *The Soteriology of Leo the Great*; B. Neil, *Leo the Great* (short summary with anthology of texts).
[70] Cf. Celestine I, *ep.* 11; Damasus, *Ad Gallos*, I, Sieben I, 810. C. Pietri, *Roma christiana* I, 528, interprets this decretal in the sense that only the bishop preached in Rome. A. Olivar, *La predicación cristiana antigua*, 530, instead has a more nuanced interpretation, even while he recognizes the supreme right of preaching went to the bishop.
[71] Cf. Sozomen, *Historia ecclesiastica* VII.19. Sozomen explains, in fact, right after this, that in Alexandria, only the bishop preached since the preaching of the priest Arius had provoked a doctrinal controversy.
[72] I discussed the Sozomen news and its implications in: E. Prinzivalli, "La comunicazione omiletica in Gregorio Magno."
[73] Leo's care in revising his homilies is comparable to that of Gregory the Great, as we know. See the just mentioned article (n. 72).

formal nature leads us to wonder whether what we have is only the part he revised attentively. The homilies, except for two cases (homily 51 on the Transfiguration and homily 95 on the Beatitudes), are not composed around a particular portion of Scripture with a line-by-line commentary, rather they are thematic in character (on the principal feasts and fasts of the year).[74] Also rare are any explicit citations of the Bible, as Leo prefers to make allusions, most likely for the sake of his style. His commitment provides us the opportunity to see how a bishop of Rome speaks to his church, to his people, and to see how much and what from the Gospel he is able or wants to transmit in that case.

Setting aside the theological and anti-heretical elements, we can see that his homilies are dominated by the overarching sense of the saving mercy of God which is offered to human beings by Jesus Christ. If we look then at the two groups of homilies in which anthropological themes, rather than doctrinal or anti-heretical ones, take the front seat—that is, the lenten homilies and those on the collections—we immediately recognize that Leo knows how to communicate the Gospel message and has thoroughly included it in his preaching. At the center of these two groups of homilies there is, on the one hand, a strong affirmation of the mercy of God, and, on the other, the call to the two-fold love of God and neighbor, with an explicit mention of the verse from the *Pater noster* ("And forgive us our debts, as we also have forgiven our debtors"). While the mention of mercy is not separated from that of the final judgement which will divide the good from the bad, it is nonetheless true that Leo reminds his listeners that it will be the lack of love which will be held against us. These are his words:

> *Sed forte sint aliqui diuitum qui, licet nullis largitionibus pauperes Ecclesiae soleant adiuuare, alia tamen Dei mandata custodiunt, et inter diuersa fidei et probitatis merita ueniabiliter sibi aestimant unam deesse uirtutem. Verum haec tanta est, ut sine illa ceterae, etiam si sint, prodesse non possint. Quamuis enim quis fidelis sit, et castus, et sobrius, et aliis moribus ornatus insignibus, si misericors tamen non est, misericordiam non meretur. Ait enim Dominus:* Beati misericordes, quoniam ipsorum miserebitur Deus (Mt 5:7). *Cum autem uenerit Filius hominis in maiestate sua et sederit in throno gloriae suae, et congregatis omnibus gentibus, bonorum et malorum fuerit facta discretio, in quo laudabuntur qui ad dexteram stabunt* (cf. Mt 25:31–46), *nisi in operibus beneuolentiae et caritatis officiis, quae Iesus Christus sibi inpensa reputabit? [. . .] Nemo igitur, dilectissimi, de ullis sibi bonae uitae meritis blandiatur, si illi defuerint opera caritatis, nec de sui corporis puritate securus sit, qui nulla elemosinarum purificatione mundatur* (cf. Lk 11:41).[75]

2. But suppose that there are some rich people who, though they are not in the habit of helping the poor in the Church with their largess, keep at any rate the commandments of God

---

74 Cf. M. Simonetti, "Esegesi e dottrina," 51–70.
75 Leo I, *Sermo* X. 2, Chavasse I, 41–43.

and figure that from among the various meritorious activities of faith they are lacking but one virtue—and it is therefore a slight fault. Yet this one virtue happens to be so important that without it the others cannot be of any avails. Be any full of faith, chaste, sober, and adorned with other noteworthy habits, yet if they are not merciful, they do not deserve mercy. For the Lord says, "Blessed are the merciful, for God will have mercy on them". When the Son of Man will come in his majesty and sit on the throne of his glory, when all nations have been gathered together, the good and the bad will be separated. What will those who are destined to stand on the right be praised for if not the benevolent works and charitable services that Jesus Christ will consider as rendered unto himself? [. . .] 3. Let none then, dearly beloved, flatter themselves about any merits due to living a good life if they lack charitable works. Nor should any be complacent about the purity of their bodies if they have not "been cleansed" al all by the purification "of alms".[76]

Leo's recommendations are placed in a social horizon of general impoverishment in which the church strengthens the usual charitable attitude: wealth is admitted but it must be directed to charity. In the words of Peter Brown: "Through the preaching of Leo, the Christian congregations were actively encouraged to view the poor as fellow members of the same urban community".[77]

The pope does not intend to dismantle the existing structures because stability must be ensured both on an economic level[78] and on that of social relations; therefore, slavery must be maintained,[79] even if managed in a Christian manner. However, it cannot be denied that his words indicate an incontrovertible primacy of charity, closely rooted in the words of Matthew.

The Beatitude addressed to the merciful is a *leitmotiv* (Mt 5:7): Leo specifies that forgiveness is first something that Christ gives,[80] but this gift must then correspond to a mutual forgiveness that forms a general habit of mercy which must be extended even to those who have not heard the Gospel.

> *In diebus igitur sanctorum ieiuniorum, pietatis opera quibus semper studendum est, abudantius exsequamur.* Misericordes simus ad omnes, maxime autem ad domesticos fidei (Lk 6:36; Gal 6:10), *ut in ipsis quoque elemosinarum distributionibus, bonitatem Patris caelestis imitemur,* qui solem suum oriri facit super bonos et malos, et pluit super iustos et iniustos (Mt 5:45). *Quamuis ergo fidelium praecipue sit adiuuanda paupertas, etiam illi tamen qui nondum euangelium receperunt, in suo labore miserandi sunt, quia in omnibus hominibus naturae est diligenda communio, quae nos etiam his benignos debet efficere, qui nobis quacumque sunt conditione subiecti, maxime si eadem gratia iam* renati (cf. Jn 3:5) *et eodem sanguinis Christi*

---

76 English translation: J.P. Freeland and A.J. Conway, *St. Leo the Great. Sermons*, 44–45.
77 P. Brown, *Through the Eye of a Needle*, 468.
78 Cf. R. Villegas Marín, "Providencia divina, desigualdad social y patronazgo aristocrático de la iglesia en la Roma de León Magno"; P. Brown, *Through the eye of a needle*, passim.
79 Cf. T. Sardella, "Schiavitù e usura," 279–287.
80 Cf. H. Feichtinger, *Die Gegenwart Christi in der Kirche bei Leo dem Grossen*, 233–242.

pretio *sunt* redempti (cf. 1 Cor 6:20). *Simul enim et cum istis habemus,* quod ad imaginem Dei conditi sumus (cf. Gen 1:27), *nec carnali origine a nobis, nec spiritali natiuitate diuisi sunt.*[81]

In these days then of the holy fast, let us pursue even more fruitfully in the works of compassion which must always be the aim of our zeal. "We must do good to all, and especially to those of the household of the faith", so that in the very distributions of alms also, we may imitate the goodness of the heavenly Father "who causes his sun to rise on good people as well as evil, and his rain to fall on the just and unjust alike". Although the poverty of the faithful ought especially to be helped, still those who have not yet received the Gospel must receive mercy in their troubles. We must love the mutual participation in human nature of all people, and it ought to make us benevolent to those also who are subject to us in whatever condition, especially if they are now reborn in the same grace, and redeemed at the same price of the blood of Christ. We have this together with them, that we are created "in the image of God", and they are not separate from us in bodily origin or in spiritual birth.[82]

I think that Leo's sense of the Gospel arises from two factors: first, the strong emphasis on the unity of nature shared by all human beings, in which the message of Genesis 1:26 ("Then God said, 'Let us make humans in our image, according to our likeness'") joined to the cosmopolitan heritage of the Stoic sort (in any case mixed with Augustinian pessimism), and second, his balanced Christology. Leo is able to represent the exquisitely human sensibility of Christ in such a way as to lead, so to say, the divine nature into taking on the concrete needs of humanity. It is not, in fact, only the movement from on high to down below—that is, of a God who saves—but also from below upwards of the one who is man and God and who manifests in the first person the aspects of piety and mercy which God asks of human beings.

This is a distillation of the teaching which Leo offers to the faithful, which maintains the imprint of the Gospel message, in a context of asceticism and the contemplation of future heavenly realities with respect to the evils of the present life. If we now turn to the four homilies *De natali ipsius*[83] delivered to the bishops gathered on the occasion of the annual anniversary of his episcopal ordination, which took place on September 29, 440, we find ourselves in a totally different atmosphere. The Petrine ideology is the clear protagonist of the narrative, expressed in a prose style that is both limpid and firm. He is the *haeres Petri in sede Petri*,[84] who represents juridically in a comprehensive way the person whose heir he is, even while recognizing his weakness and personal unworthiness (*Sermo* II.1), for which he confides himself to the support of God:

---

[81] Leo I, *Sermo* XLI.3, Chavasse II, 235–236.
[82] English translation: J.P. Freeland and A.J. Conway, *St. Leo the Great. Sermons*, 178.
[83] Leo I, *Sermo* II, III, IV, V, Chavasse I, 7–25.
[84] Leo I, *Sermo* II.2, Chavasse I, 8, 35–39. Cf. *Sermo* III.4.

> *De uestro itaque et ipse gaudet (scil. Petrus) affectu et in consortibus honoris sui obseruantiam dominicae institutionis amplectitur, probans ordinatissimam totius Ecclesiae caritatem quae in Petri sede Petrum suscipit et a tanti amore pastoris nec in persona tam inparis tepescit heredis.*

> He too rejoices in your affection. He embraces the observance instituted by our Lord among those who have a share in his honor. He approves the very well-ordered charity in the entire Church, which receives as Peter the one who occupies his see and which does not grow lukewarm in its love for so great shepherd, not even in the person of so inferior an heir.[85]

It is precisely on the figure of Peter, whose heir he is, that Leo concentrates in order to amass support for the many arguments in favor of Roman primacy. To the words of Jesus in Mt 16:18–19, understood according to the now-established Roman tradition, he adds a complete portrait of the person of Peter (*Sermo* III.2; IV.2), beginning with his response to Jesus (Mt 16:16): *Tu es Christus filius Dei uiui* ("You are the Christ, the Son of the living God").[86] The confession of Peter legitimizes, for Leo, the universal teaching office of the Roman Church: *In uniuersa namque Ecclesia, Tu es Christus Filius Dei uiui cotidie Petrus dicit, et omnis lingua quae Dominum confitetur* (cf. Rom 14:11) *magisterio huius imbuitur*[87] ("In the universal Church, Peter says every day 'You are the Christ, Son of the living God.' Therefore, throughout the whole Church, Peter says: 'You are the Christ, the Son of the living God,' 'every tongue that confesses the Lord' has been imbued with the teaching of his utterance").[88] Peter is constantly[89] singled out for Jesus's attention, and Leo makes use, for good reason, of the words of Jesus found only in Lk 22:31–32: *Simon, Simon, ecce Satanas expostulauit ut uos cerneret uelut triticum. Ego autem rogaui pro te, ne deficiat fides tua. Et tu conuersus confirma fratres tuos ne intretis in temptationem* ("Simon, Simon, behold, Satan has obtained his request to sift you [all] like wheat. I, however, have begged for you that your faith not fail. Once you have converted, strengthen your brethren, lest you [all] enter into temptation"). In these words, the brethren (the Apostles) are involved in a situation in which they receive confirmation in the Faith by Peter. Leo does not deny that the *ius potestatis istius* is passed on to all the Apostles, but he does reaffirm the Petrine primacy. In the fourth sermon, given in 444, while in Rome all were discussing an incident provoked by Hilarius of Arles, Leo includes words which

---

[85] English translation: J.P. Freeland and A.J. Conway, *St. Leo the Great. Sermons*, 20. Cf. *Sermo* III.4.
[86] It is Matthew who adds the divine Filiation to the messianic profession of Mk 8:29 and Lk 9:20.
[87] Leo I, *Sermo* III.3, Chavasse I, 13, 75–77.
[88] English translation: J.P. Freeland and A.J. Conway, *St. Leo the Great. Sermons*, 23.
[89] Cf. Leo I, *Sermo* IV.3.4, Chavasse I, 19–20. 21; *Sermo* LXXXIII, 3, Chavasse II, 45–48.

he had spoken already in a sermon given just months before for the feast of St. Peter (*Sermo* LXXXIII.2):

> *Manet ergo Petri priuilegium, ubicumque ex ipsius fertur aequitate iudicium. Nec nimia est uel seueritas, uel remissio, ubi nihil erit ligatum, nihil solutum, nisi quod beatus Petrus aut soluerit aut ligarit.*[90]

> Therefore, this privilege of Peter resides wherever judgment has been passed in accordance with his fairness. There cannot be too much severity or too much lenience where nothing is bound or loosed outside of that which blessed Peter has loosed or bound.[91]

---

90 Leo I, *Sermo* IV.3, Chavasse I, 19,88–20,91.
91 English translation: J.P. Freeland and A.J. Conway, *St. Leo the Great. Sermons*, 28.

Conclusion

What can we conclude from this discussion beginning with *First Letter of Clement* and arriving at Boniface the First, to which we have also joined Leo the Great, in a rapid and partial, if significant, comparison? For sure, the most characteristic words from the teachings of Jesus do not seem to be the ones most adept to ground the foundational theory of an institution, regardless of whatever institution we might consider. In fact, an institution does not need only to presuppose its indefinite duration but also to place itself as the supreme authority. Thus, the apocalyptic face and potentially subversive message of Jesus was translated into a reference to a future, heavenly reign to which one has access by means of a certain way of life, the goodness of which was certified by ecclesiastical authority. In the end, the words of Jesus chosen were those suitable to be used to confirm the authority of the institutional Church, which would come to have the result of a clear and immediate precept or even a warning tone capable of producing fear. The heart of the Gospel, however, is not there. Yet, Jesus's words of love and forgiveness were not forgotten, as we have seen. Even at the distance of centuries, Leo, in his preaching to the faithful, shows that he has not forgotten them. Nonetheless, with the bishops he uses a different tone and calls on Jesus's words to Peter which legitimize his own authority. This is opposed to what we saw with Zosimus, who in the first phase of his interaction with the African bishops tried to recall the words of Jesus on the love of neighbor. To address those words to an episcopacy convinced they were in the right could of course have no positive effect.

So too in the case of the Roman interpretation of Jesus's words to Peter which came to nothing when a pope did not agree with the intentions of a given episcopate. The resilience of the popes of the Rome, however, was one of the factors of their success throughout this long period. Hammering away at the same point—the words of Mt 16:18–19 according to the Roman interpretation—and trusting that eventually the reality would progressively align with the theory, it did come true, at least for a part of Christianity.

Bibliography

Abbreviations

Sieben I–III = Sieben, Hermann-Josef, ed. *Vetustissimae epistulae Romanorum pontificum*. FC 58, 1–3. Freiburg/ Basel/ Vienna: Herder, 2014–2015.

Chavasse I–II = *Sancti Leonis Magni Romani Pontificis Tractatus septem et nonaginta*, recensuit Antonius Chavasse (CCSL CXXXVIII-CXXXVIII A). Turnhout: Brepols 1973.

Further abbreviations follow IATG (Siegfried Schwertner. *Internationales Abkürzungsverzeichnis für Theologie und Grenzgebiete*. Berlin/Boston: De Gruyter ³2014).

Primary Sources

Chavasse, Antoine, ed. *Sancti Leonis Magni Romani Pontificis Tractatus septem et nonaginta*, CCSL CXXXVIII-CXXXVIII A. Turnhout: Brepols, 1973.

Hartel, Wilhelm, ed. *Cyprianus, Opera omnia (pars II)*: *Epistulae*. CSEL 3/2. Vienna: [Verlag der österreichischen Akademie der Wissenschaften], 1871.

Sieben, Hermann-Josef, ed. *Vetustissimae epistulae Romanorum pontificum*. FC 58/1–3. Freiburg/ Basel/ Vienna: Herder, 2014–2015.

Thompson, Glen L. *The Correspondence of Pope Julius I. Greek and Latin Text and English Translation with Introduction and Commentary*. LEC 3. Washington, D.C.: The Catholic University of America Press, 2015.

Literature

Abramowski, Luise. "Dionys von Rom († 268) und Dionys von Alexandrien († 264/5) in den arianischen Streitigkeiten des 4. Jahrhunderts." *Zeitschrift für Kirchengeschichte* 93 (1982): 240–272. English translation: "Dionysius of Rome (d. 268) and Dionysius of Alexandria (d. 264/5) in the Arian Controversies of the Fourth Century." In Ead. *Formula and Context. Studies in Early Christian Thought*, no. 11, London: Ashgate, 1992.

Aguirre, Rafael. "La segunda generación y la conservación de la memoria de Jesús." In Id., ed. *Así empezó el cristianismo*, 195–254. Estella: Editorial Verbo Divino, 2010.

Aguirre, Rafael. "Jesús y el tiempo." In Garribba, Dario, ed. *Costruzioni del tempo nelle prime comunità cristiane*. Atti del XVII Convegno di Studi Neotestamentari. Venezia, 14–16 Settembre 2017, *Ricerche storico-bibliche* 31/2 (2019): 93–112.

Allison, Dale Clifford Jr. *Jesus of Nazareth. Millenarian Prophet*. Minneapolis: Fortress Press, 1998.

Allison, Dale Clifford Jr. *Constructing Jesus. Memory, Imagination, and History*. Grand Rapids: Baker Academic, 2010.

Armitage, Mark J. *A Twofold Solidarity: Leo the Great's Theology of Redemption*. Early Christian Studies (St Pauls) 9. Strathfield: St Pauls Publications, 2005.

Assmann, Jan. *Das kulturelle Gedächtnis. Schrift, Erinnerung und politische Identität in frühen Hochkulturen*. Beck: Munich, 1992. English Translation: *Cultural Memory and Early Civilization: Writing, Remembrance, and Political Imagination*. Cambridge: Cambridge University Press, 2012.

Babut, Ernest-Charles. *La plus ancien décrétale*. Paris: Société nouvelle de librairie et d'édition, 1904.

Berno, Francesco. *L'Atto di Pietro e le origini della comunità cristiana di Roma*. Rome: Carocci, 2022.

Bovon, François. *Das Evangelium nach Lukas. 1. Teilband. Lk 1,1–9,50*. EKK Evangelisch-Katholischer Kommentar III/1. Zurich: Benziger Verlag, 1989.

Brown, Peter. *Through the Eye of a Needle: Wealth, the Fall of Rome, and the Making of Christianity in the West, 350–550 AD*. Princeton, N.J./ Oxford: Princeton University Press, 2012.

Bruner, Jason. *How to Study Global Christianity: A Short Guide for Students*. London: Palgrave Macmillan, 2022.

Butticaz, Simon, and Enrico Norelli, eds. *Memory and Memories in Early Christianity. Proceedings of the International Conference held at the Universities of Geneva and Lausanne (June 2–3, 2016)*. WUNT 398. Tübingen: Mohr Siebeck, 2018.

Byrskog, Samuel. *Story as History—History as Story. The Gospel Tradition in the Context of Ancient Oral History*. WUNT 123. Tübingen: Mohr Siebeck, 2000.

Canella, Tessa, ed. "La Memoria e l'Immagine. Linguaggio, testi e cultura visuale nella costruzione delle memorie culturali cristiane tardoantiche (III–VII sec.)." *Rivista di Storia del Cristianesimo* 20/2 (2023) 227–402.

Castelli, Emanuele. "Dati storici e aspetti romanzeschi nelle prime due Visioni del Pastore di Erma. Una riconsiderazione del problema alla luce di nuove scoperte testuali." *Augustinianum* 60 (2020): 321–340.

Castelli, Emanuele. "Gli esordi alternativi del *Pastore* di Erma." *Adamantius* 26 (2020): 551–575.

Clarke, Graeme Wilber, ed. *The Letters of St. Cyprian of Carthage*. ACW 47. New York, N.Y/Mahwah, N.J: Newman Press, 1989.

Czachesz, István, ed. "Network Science in Biblical Studies." *Annali di Storia dell'Esegesi* 39/1 (2022): 9–180.

Destro, Adriana, and Mauro Pesce. *Encounters with Jesus: the Man in His Place and Time*. Minneapolis: Fortress Press, 2011 [orig. Milan 2008].

Di Capua, Francesco. "Da Siricio a Sisto III." In Id., *Il ritmo prosaico nelle lettere dei papi e nei documenti della Cancelleria romana dal IV al XIV secolo*, Lateranum, N.S. 2.3.4, vol. II, 143–161; 205–214.

Di Pasquale, Caterina. *Antropologia della memoria. Il ricordo come fatto culturale*. Bologna: Il Mulino, 2017.

Duval, Yves-Marie. *La décrétale Ad Gallos Episcopos: son texte et son auteur. Texte critique, traduction française et commentaire*. SVigChr 73. Leiden/Boston: Brill 2005.

Esler, Philip Francis. *Conflict and Identity in Romans. The Social Setting of Paul's Letter*. Minneapolis: Augsburg Fortress, 2003.

Feichtinger, Hans. *Die Gegenwart Christi in der Kirche bei Leo dem Grossen*. Pat 18. Frankfurt a. Main: P. Lang, 2007.

Fiano, Emanuel. *Three Powers in Heaven. The Emergence of Theology and the Parting of the Ways*. New Haven/London: Yale University Press, 2023.

Firth, David G., and Philip S. Johnston, eds. *Interpreting Deuteronomy: Issues and Approaches*. Downers Grove (IL): InterVarsity, 2012.

Freeland, Jane Patricia, and Agnes Josephine Conway, eds. *St. Leo the Great. Sermons*. The Fathers of the Church 93. Washington, D.C: The Catholic University of America Press, 1996.

Green, Bernard. *The Soteriology of Leo the Great*, Oxford: Oxford University Press, 2008.

Halbwachs, Maurice. *Les cadres sociaux de la mémoire*. Paris: Albin Michel, 1994 [orig. 1925].
Harkins, Angela Kim. "Entering the Narrative World of Hermas's Visions." In Ead., and Harry O. Maier, eds. *Experiencing the Shepherd of Hermas*, 117–136. Ekstasis 10. Berlin/Boston: De Gruyter, 2022.
Institutum Patristicum Augustinianum, ed. *La memoria. Forme e finalità del ricordare nel cristianesimo antico*. XLVIII Incontro di Studiosi dell'Antichità cristiana. Roma, 5–7 maggio 2022. SEAug 164. Rome/Florence: Institutum Patristicum Augustinianum- Nerbini International, 2023.
Jenkins, Philip. *The Next Christendom. The Coming of Global Christianity*. Oxford: Oxford University Press, 2002.
Jenkins, Philip. *The New Faces of Christianity: Believing the Bible in the Global South*. Oxford: Oxford University Press, 2006.
Kampmann, Claudia, Ulrich Volp, Martin Wallraff, and Julia Winnebeck, eds. *Kirchengeschichte. Historisches Spezialgebiet und/ oder Theologische Disziplin, Theologie, Kultur*. Hermeneutik 28. Leipzig: Evangelische Verlagsanstalt, 2020.
Lamberigts, Mathijs. "Was Innocent Familiar with the Content of the Pelagian Controversy? A Study of his Answers to the Letters sent by the African Episcopacy." In Nehring, Przemysław, Mateusz Stróżyński, and Rafał Toczko, eds. *Scrinium Augustini. The World of Augustine's Letters*. IPM 76. 203–223. Turnhout: Brepols, 2017.
Lampe, Peter. *From Paul to Valentinus: Christians at Rome in the First Two Centuries*, ed. by M.D. Johnson, Minneapolis (Mn): Fortress Press, 2003.
MacDonald, Margaret Y., and Carolyn Osiek. *A Woman's Place. House Churches in Earliest Christianity*. Minneapolis: Fortress Press, 2006.
Marcos, Mar. "Papal Authority, Local Autonomy and Imperial Control: Pope Zosimus and the Western Churches (a. 417–18)." In Fear, Andrew, José Fernández Ubiña, and Mar Marcos, eds. *The Role of the Bishop in Late Antiquity. Conflict and Compromise*. 145–166, London: Bloomsbury, 2013.
Markschies, Christoph. *Gottes Körper. Jüdische, christliche und pagane Gottesvorstellungen in der Antike*. München: C.H. Beck, 2016. English Translation by Alexander Johannes Edmonds: *God's Body. Jewish, Christian and Pagan Images of God*. Waco TX: Baylor University Press, 2019.
Meier, John P. *A Marginal Jew. Rethinking the Historical Jesus. II. Mentor, Message, and Miracles*, New York: Anchor Bible Reference Library, 1994.
Monaci, Adele, and Andrea Nicolotti, eds. "Vedere e guardare attraverso le parole: contributi per una storia della cultura visuale del cristianesimo antico e tardoantico." *Adamantius* 26 (2020): 6–319.
Neil, Bronwen. *Leo the Great*. The Early Church Fathers. London: Routledge, 2009.
Norelli, Enrico. "Dai presbiteri d'asia agli episcopi di Roma secondo Ireneo di Lione. Parte I." *Augustinianum* 73/1 (2023), 9–45 and "Parte II." *Augustinianum* 73/2 (2023): 9–45.
Norelli, Enrico. *Il corpus attribuito a Ippolito*, in C. Moreschini—E. Norelli, *Storia della letteratura cristiana antica greca e latina. I: Da Paolo all'età costantiniana*. New revised and expanded edition, Morcelliana, Brescia 2019, 432–484.
Olivar, Alexandre. *La predicación cristiana antigua*. Biblioteca Herder. Sección de teología y filosofía 189. Barcelona: Herder, 1991.
Pesce, Mauro. "Alla ricerca di un nuovo schema mentale. Appunti utili anche per la linea editoriale di *Annali di Storia dell'Esegesi* nei prossimi anni." *Annali di Storia dell'Esegesi* 40/1 (2023): 13–40.
Pidolle, Laurent. *La christologie historique du pape saint Léon le Grand*. Cogitatio fidei 290. Paris: Cerf, 2013.
Pietri, Charles. *Roma christiana. Recherches sur l'Église de Rome, son organisation, sa politique, son idéologie de Miltiade à Sixte III (311–440)*, 2 vol. Bibliothèque des écoles françaises d'Athènes et de Rome 224. Rome: Ecole française de Rome, 1976.

Prinzivalli, Emanuela. "La comunicazione omiletica in Gregorio Magno." In *Gregorio Magno nel XIV centenario della morte*. Roma, 22–25 ottobre 2003. Atti dei Convegni Lincei, 209, Rome: Accademia dei Lincei 2004, 153–170, repr. in Ead., *Il cristianesimo antico fra tradizioni e traduzioni*, 81–102.

Prinzivalli, Emanuela. "La componente patristica." In Ufficio delle celebrazioni liturgiche del Sommo Pontefice, ed. *Inizio del ministero petrino del vescovo di Roma Benedetto XVI*, 191–207. Vatican City: Libreria Editrice Vaticana, 2006.

Prinzivalli, Emanuela. "La prima lettera di Clemente ai Corinzi." In Ead., and Manlio Simonetti, eds. *Seguendo Gesù. Testi cristiani delle origini*, I, 79–275; 449–541. Milan: Fondazione Lorenzo Valla—Mondadori, 2010.

Prinzivalli, Emanuela. *Il cristianesimo antico fra tradizioni e traduzioni*. Fundamentis novis 7. Rome: Città Nuova, 2019.

Prinzivalli, Emanuela. "Anastasio I di Roma e le lettere ai vescovi di Milano sulla condanna di Origene." *Cristianesimo nella storia* 42 (2021): 7–28.

Prinzivalli, Emanuela. "Amate pacem, diligite caritatem, studete concordiam. Quando il papa sbaglia: Celestio e Pelagio tra Innocenzo I e Zosimo." In Barcellona, Rossana, and Arianna Rotondo, eds. *Protagonisti e antagonisti del Primato. Cristianesimo Poteri Istituzioni. Studi per Teresa Sardella*, 51–88. Armarium 18. Soveria Mannelli: Rubbettino, 2022.

Rebillard, Éric. "Sociologie de la déviance et orthodoxie. Le cas de la controversepélagienne sur la grâce." In Elm, Susanna, Éric Rebillard, and Antonella Romano, eds. *Orthodoxie, christianisme, histoire*, 221–240. Rome: École française, 2000.

Reutter, Ursula. *Damasus, Bischof von Rom (366–384): Leben und Werke*. STAC 55. Tübingen: Mohr Siebeck, 2009.

Ruggieri, Giuseppe. *La zizzania nella chiesa e nel mondo. Interpretazioni di una parabola*. CrSt 26/1. Bologna: EDB, 2005.

Sacchi, Paolo. *Storia del Secondo Tempio. Israele tra VI secolo a.C. e I secolo d.C.* Nuova edizione a cura di Luca Mazzinghi. Presentazione di Romano Penna. Turin: Claudiana, 2019.

Sardella, Teresa. "Schiavitù e usura: diritto di proprietà e ricchezza illecita nella codificazione ecclesiastica (Leone papa, ep. 4, cann.1-3-4)." In *Povertà e ricchezza nel cristianesimo antico (I–V sec.). XLII Incontro di Studiosi dell'Antichità Cristiana*, 279–287. Rome: Institutum Patristicum Augustinianum, 2016.

Schatz, Klaus. *Papal Primacy. From its Origins to the Present*. trans. from German by John A. Otto and Linda M. Maloney. Collegeville, Minn.: The Liturgical Press, 1996 [orig. Würzburg 1990].

Scott, Joan W. "Gender. A Useful Category of Historical Analysis." *The American Historical Review* 41/5 (1986): 1055–1075.

Scott, Joan W. "Unanswered Questions. AHR Forum. Revisiting 'Gender. A Useful Category of Historical Analysis'." *The American Historical Review* 113/5 (2008): 1422–1430.

Simonetti, Manlio. "Aspetti della cristologia del III secolo. Dionigi di Alessandria." In *La Cristologia nei Padri della Chiesa. Bessarionaea* (Academia Cardinalis Bessarionis 7). Rome: Herder 1989, 37–65, repr. in Id., *Studi sulla cristologia del II e III secolo*. Studia Ephemeridis Augustinianum 44. Rome: Institutum Patristicum Augustinianum, 1993, 289–292.

Simonetti, Manlio. "Esegesi e dottrina." In Naldini, Mario, ed. *I sermoni di Leone Magno fra storia e teologia*. Prefazione di Gianfranco Ravasi. Fiesole: Nardini, 1997, 51–70.

Simonetti, Manlio. "Il *Pastore* di Erma." In Prinzivalli, Emanuela, and Manlio Simonetti, eds. *Seguendo Gesù. Testi cristiani delle origini*. II. 179–489; 550–592. Milan: Fondazione Lorenzo Valla—Mondadori, 2015.

Smith, Eric C. *Foucault's Heterotopia in Christian Catacombs. Constructing Spaces and Symbols in Ancient Rome*. New York: Palgrave Macmillan, 2014.

Theissen, Gert. *Die Jesusbewegung. Sozialgeschichte einer Revolution der Werte*. Gütersloh: Gütersloher Verlagshaus, 2004.

Urciuoli, Emiliano Rubens. *La religione urbana. Come la città ha prodotto il cristianesimo*. Prefazione di Mauro Pesce. Bologna: EDB, 2021.

Villegas Marín, Raúl. "Providencia divina, desigualidad social y patronazgo aristocrático de la iglesia en la Roma de León Magno." In *Povertà e ricchezza nel cristianesimo antico*. XLII Incontro di Studiosi dell'Antichità Cristiana. Roma, 8–10 maggio 2014, 289–309. Rome: Institutum Patristicum Augustinianum, 2016.

Weckwerth, Andreas. "The Twenty Canons of the Council of Nicaea." In Kim, Young Richard, ed. *The Cambridge Companion to the Council of Nicaea*, 158–176. Cambridge: Cambridge University Press, 2021.

Wessel, Susan. *Leo the Great and the Spiritual Rebuilding of a Universal Rome*. SVigChr 93. Leiden/Boston: Brill, 2008.

www.ingramcontent.com/pod-product-compliance
Lightning Source LLC
Chambersburg PA
CBHW020423230426
43663CB00007BA/1286